DESIGN
&
TECHNOLOGY

DESIGN
&
TECHNOLOGY
ERASING
THE
BOUNDARIES

Wendy Richmond

. . . .

VNR Van Nostrand Reinhold
New York

Library of Congress Catalog Card Number 90-12024
ISBN 0-442-00409-5

Printed in the United States of America

Van Nostrand Reinhold
115 Fifth Avenue
New York, New York 10003

Van Nostrand Reinhold International Company Limited
11 New Fetter Lane
London EC4P 4EE, England

Van Nostrand Reinhold
480 La Trobe Street
Melbourne, Victoria 3000, Australia

Nelson Canada
1120 Birchmount Road
Scarborough, Ontario M1K 5G4, Canada

16 15 14 13 12 11 10 9 8 7 6 5 4 3 2 1

Library of Congress Cataloging-in-Publication Data

Richmond, Wendy.
     Design & technology : erasing the boundaries / Wendy Richmond.
          p.   cm.
     ISBN 0-442-00409-5
     1. Printing, Practical--Layout--Data processing. 2. Computer
graphics. I. Title. II. Title: Design and technology.
     Z246.R4 1990   90-12024
     686.2'25--dc20   CIP

For my mother

Contents

PREFACE · *IX*

1 · IMAGESETTERS · *1*

2 · DIGITAL TYPE MASTERS · *5*

3 · POINTING DEVICES · *10*

4 · CAPTURED KEYSTROKES · *14*

5 · TRADE SHOWS · *19*

6 · RESOLUTION · *22*

7 · THE ELECTRONIC WORKFLOW · *26*

8 · MANY TOOLS, ONE BOX · *29*

9 · INCREASING IDEA TIME · *32*

10 · QUICK CORRECTIONS · *35*

11 · GREETINGS FROM DESIGN · *38*

12 · TIME TO BUY? · *42*

13 · TYPE DESIGN · *47*

14 · ELECTRONIC RENTAL STUDIOS · *52*

15 · DESIGN MANAGEMENT · *55*

16 · DISK CRASHES · *60*

17 · REALISTIC EXPECTATIONS · *63*

18 · TYPE FOR ENVIRONMENTAL DESIGN · *68*

19 · VARIED TASKS · *77*

20 · A DEDICATED SYSTEM · *81*

21 · REAL TYPE · *85*

22 · KEEPING UP WITH YOUR CLIENTS · *88*

23 · LAST YEAR'S BUDGET · *91*

24 · SYSTEM INCOMPATIBILITY · *94*

25 · CONSIDER VIDEO · *98*

26 · ERASING THE BOUNDARIES · *101*

27 · POSTERS OF THE FUTURE · *106*

28 · HOT AND COLD MEDIA · *109*

29 · THE DESIGN PROCESS · *112*

30 · THE BUSINESS SIDE · *115*

31 · DESIGN TOOLS · *118*

32 · DESIGN TECHNOLOGY SURVEY · *123*

33 · SURVEY RESULTS · *126*

34 · POOR SHOPPING · *140*

35 · COMMISSION A TYPEFACE · *144*

36 · EDUCATING YOUR CLIENTS · *147*

37 · COMPUTERS IN THE STUDIO · *150*

38 · THE BOTTOM LINE · *171*

39 · MULTIMEDIA · *175*

40 · INTERACTIVE MEDIA · *180*

APPENDIX A · *187*

APPENDIX B · *191*

CREDITS · *199*

INDEX · *202*

Preface

IN 1984, RICHARD COYNE, editor and publisher of *Communication Arts* magazine, asked me to write a column about new technology. In his introduction, Dick said, "This is the first in a series of columns that will appear regularly in *CA*. Wendy will report on and explain the existing processes, equipment, and new developments in the area of computer graphics and computer-aided design and production."

Every year since then, the mission has grown. The technology we now have certainly existed six years ago, but it was too expensive for us to buy or use and was therefore remote. Over the years, the technology has migrated to equipment that's affordable and that answers the specific needs of the designer. This book is a chronological collection of columns and articles, including one from *Step-by-Step Graphics,* spanning that six-year period.

Looking back, I find that the first year's columns are perhaps more important to read today than they were at the time, because now we're using the tools. The columns explain what the technology is and what you can do with it. They'll give you an understanding of the new tools and provide a basis for learning about new developments.

The next two years of columns (1985 and 1986) show the successes, frustrations, and unexpected experiences of designers who were just beginning to use and investigate computer-based tools. More control, speed, and economy could be gained with new tools. But the software available had severe limitations, such as the lack of typographic features and the limited typeface selection. How long can one stomach a diet of unkerned Times and Helvetica?

My message was "Don't lose hope." A problem that can be

Design and Technology

articulated is practically solved. Sure enough, the control that we found lacking then is now abundant. In fact, we have access to features that we didn't even know we wanted! By 1987 computers were accepted as a desirable addition to the studio. Designers were ready to buy. Many of the columns after this point, as well as an appendix of resource listings and another of acronyms, include practical advice on buying and using computers.

When you become comfortable with new tools, you begin to ponder deeper, less tangible concerns that arise only with experience. "How do computers affect the design process? How will visual communication be distributed in the future, when computer terminals are in our homes? What new avenues do computers open for the profession of design, and for me?" The columns that explored these subjects were important then; they are even more important now, as computers multiply not only in studios, but in design schools as well.

In 1988 Dick and I decided that it was time for a survey. I wrote a questionnaire, and we received extensive answers from design professionals across the country. The questionnaire and the survey results, showing what designers are buying, spending, using, and thinking about computers, are included in this book.

These responses, along with subsequent columns, reveal the changing relationships between different designers, designers and suppliers, and designers and clients. We are still asking these questions: "Am I a typesetter? Should I be looking for new suppliers who are more computer-literate? What about my staff? Will I hire more or fire more? How do I deal with clients who have their own computers and want to produce their own mechanicals?"

Several longer articles are case studies about established designers who are neck-deep in computers, with realistic views of the pros and cons. Not surprisingly, their conclusions are unanimous: Now that they are comfortable with computers, they can't imagine life without them.

Finally, the book explores new media. When we first met computers, we thought of them only as new tools to replace older ones.

Preface

As computers become ubiquitous, even invisible, in our television sets, our CD players, and our telephones, we will use the computer not only as a tool to produce visual communication, but also as a medium for receiving and interacting with visual communication. Designers have the opportunity and the challenge to design for a new medium.

Through real experiences and descriptions, this book provides a basic understanding of computer-based tools for the design professional. I hope it helps you to bring these exciting creatures into your professional lives, and inspires you to explore new avenues for your creative energies.

►WE NEED TO

erase the boundaries

between designer and

consumer, between print

and video, between problem

solving and invention.

Imagesetters

Designers rarely see the typesetters, typositors, and other machines that produce the tangible ingredients of their work. It's not surprising that the mental images of those machines are sometimes out of date. Those in the graphic arts industry who purchase production equipment are quite the opposite; the pictures in their heads are blueprints for the future.

Imagesetters can greatly reduce and consolidate the number of steps required to produce the mechanical for the printed page. They promise to whittle down the tasks of pasteup as well as film combination and stripping.

What is an imagesetter?

It's a machine that sets images. The generality of its name is very much in keeping with what this device is capable of setting. We could call it a thingsetter. "Things" are type, rules, line art, halftones, tint screens—basically, any element that you would find on a mechanical for a page to be printed. Currently, these things are produced on a variety of machines. A typesetting machine produces the text, type, and rules. A typositor produces the headline type. A reproduction camera produces the photostats of line art at requested reductions or enlargements and produces halftones from continuous-tone black-and-white photographs. The resulting products of type, line art, and halftones are collected, trimmed, made sticky, and pasted onto a common ground. An imagesetter can produce all of the above items on a single piece of reproduction paper or film.

That's impressive. But the more significant aspect of imagesetting is its ability to eliminate steps in the process that presently require expensive time and materials; that is, physically combining the items on a page that reverse out, crop, or in any other way integrate with each other. The complex set of steps required to produce layers of negatives and overlays consumes time and materials. An imagesetter performs these tasks internally and mathematically, creating the proper reverses, combining tint screens with typography, cropping halftone illustrations with precise shapes—all to come out in position as a single piece of reproduction material.

How does an imagesetter work?

An imagesetter "draws" all items of the page (typographic elements, line art, and halftones) the same way, as rows of extremely small dots. This method of making shapes out of the smallest possible elements (which is as old as mosaic, needlework, and tapestry) provides a precise way of describing a shape. "On this regular pattern, put these dots in and leave these dots out." In typesetting technology, for example, characters have long since ceased to exist as visible shapes stored in the typesetter. Instead, they are stored as sets of instructions. A beam of light traverses light-sensitive paper or film and turns on and off as it is instructed by the computer. Put this dot in; leave this dot out. Eventually (meaning in fractions of a second) character shapes are formed, made up of a series of tiny, slightly overlapping dots.

These dots need not be limited to forming a typographic shape. Many small dots can form individual irregular shapes in a mezzotint screen, line art illustrations, et cetera. And these dots can form the shapes that are created when type drops out of line art, or a halftone is cropped by a circle. The key here is to envision type, line art, and halftones, and their possible integrations, as a collection of shapes made up of same-sized dots. This allows an imagesetter to represent all "things," regardless of what one may choose to call them.

Where are imagesetters?

In the graphic arts industry, most new technology is developed to enhance productivity. Large newspapers and magazines, where production is heavy and primarily in-house, are the adventurous initial investors in this new technology. Because the entire production process is under their control, an ideal environment is provided in which to measure the cost-effectiveness and efficiency of imagesetting.

How will imagesetters affect graphic designers?

Printers, type shops, and other production suppliers are watching and in some cases purchasing this new technology. Although graphic designers are physically remote from these devices, much of the material they receive is still hot from some computer's current.

Graphic designers' suppliers have become multipurpose. Printers set type, typesetters make stats, and stat houses develop photographic prints. State-of-the-art equipment that combines tasks can be cost-justified. Your favorite typesetter could, in the near future, own an imagesetter. Does that mean that you could discard your scissors and rubber cement? Is this the end of many-layered mechanicals with as many sets of registration marks?

Maybe. Although an imagesetter is capable of setting type, line art, and halftones at the location, size, and rotation needed for a mechanical, it requires specifications that tell it where, how big, and at what angle. The fact that a machine has the capability to set all items in position means that the instructions must be explicit—as explicit as a mechanical. The greater the amount of drudgery one expects a machine to eliminate, the more specific the instructions must be.

Currently, operators of typesetters must enter complicated markup codes into the "front end," the machine that electronically sends

Design and Technology

typographic instructions to the typesetting machine. The multitude of codes necessary to imageset a complex page is overwhelming. How will operators enter instructions into the "front end" of an imagesetter?

Fortunately, the burden of entering special codes is being lifted from the operator's shoulders. Instead, the "front ends" sending instructions to a setter of any sort are becoming more visual. The operator can construct an actual page on a video screen, and the underlying specifications are stored and/or automatically sent to the imagesetter.

How will graphic designers send specifications to their suppliers? Will they continue to give suppliers written instructions or will they, too, use machines to construct "intermediate" pages visually on screens?

Just as inquiries and needs of the production industry have influenced production technology, so will graphic designers influence graphic design technology. New tools someday will allow designers to take full advantage of imagesetters.

◆ Update: Today, designers can choose from thousands of software programs and service bureaus to create, combine, and set all of the elements for the printed page.

Digital
Type Masters

Graphic designers dictate the place-
ment of typographic form but, for the most part, do not control
the shapes of the characters themselves. The shapes, replicated from
typographic masters, are defined long before they reach the type
shops. Most typesetting companies have developed digital typesetters, and have created digital type masters.

What are digital type masters?

A character master in some digital typesetters is a shape made
up of a regular pattern of dots. The dots are stored in the typesetter as *bitmaps:* a list of numbers locating their position in the character shape. Because the dot size in the typesetter remains constant, larger characters are made up of more dots than are smaller
characters. Therefore, each point size requires an individual master. To typeset a digital character, a single beam of light sweeps across
light-sensitive paper in a series of parallel lines (in most, about 1,000
lines per inch), turning on and off to expose dots according to each
character's list.

The computers in digital typesetters have a large capacity for storing numbers, but the vast number of dots needed to represent every character of an alphabet in every desired point size restricts the number of typefaces that can be stored on a typesetter at one time. In order to increase the storage capacity, more economical methods for describing a digital master have been developed. Character shapes are primarily large areas of black and white, which can be described as filled-in outlines. Rather than list the location of every dot in a character shape, closely spaced dots along the outline can be stored and connected by very short straight lines. When the character is typeset, the outline is filled in with dots. A digital type master in this form is then enlarged and reduced to produce multiple point sizes. But as the master is enlarged, so are the straight lines, and curves that were smooth begin to break up. Thus, additional larger masters with short lines are needed to produce a variety of point sizes.

A third, more efficient technique for storing digital type masters involves storing only specific dots along the outline. These dots, or *control points,* define the curves and straight lines of the character's outline. The spacing of the control points determines the shape of each curve. Control points also mark the beginning and end of a straight line. The characters reside in the typesetter in this abbreviated form; neither the shape nor the outline is "drawn" until the character is typeset. Therefore, one master's control points can represent any size character with perfectly smooth curves.

How are digital type masters created?

In order to store a character shape as either a bitmap, outline dots, or control points on an outline, the original artwork must be translated into a corresponding digital form. To translate a shape into a bitmap or an outline of dots, a drawing of the character or an enlargement of an existing typeset character is *scanned—* photographed by a camera that records the shape as a pattern of dots. But scanning presents problems. Original drawings of typefaces are usually unavailable, and enlargements of typeset copy are uneven and therefore unacceptable shapes. Extensive hand editing of the resulting dots is necessary to create a reasonable alphabet.

Storing the control points of a character's shape requires a different process. The accompanying photographs illustrate the production process of Bitstream Inc., a digital type foundry that creates digital type masters in the form of control points for a variety of digital typesetters and imagesetters. The electronic workstations used by Bitstream lettering artists are produced by Camex, Inc.; the programs described were developed by the designers and programmers of the two companies.

Before beginning the production of a typeface, Bitstream studies character weights and widths, and corrects individual characters to take advantage of new technology. Character masters were once widened or squeezed to fit limited spacing increments on various unit systems; digital typesetters are capable of precisely reproducing the original design intention.

▶Using an electronic puck, the lettering artist specifies control points along the character's outline. The control points define the shape of the character.

Lettering artists experienced in specifying control points mark the points' locations on enlargements of typeset characters or strips of film. The artwork is placed on the workstation's digitizing tablet. By placing an electronic *puck* over the marks and pushing the puck's *select* button, the locations of the points are recorded. As each point is entered, it appears on the screen of the workstation. The points on the screen can be moved at any time during the production process to perfect the character's shape.

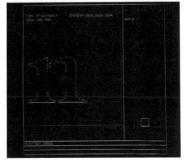

▶Once all of an individual character's points have been recorded, the resulting shape automatically appears on the screen.

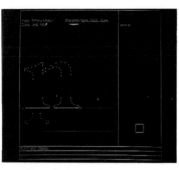 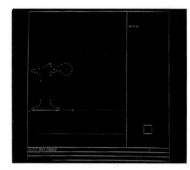

After all the points on an individual character have been entered, an outline is drawn to show the resulting shape. The points can be temporarily turned off in order to see the outline more clearly.

Character parts such as stems and serifs repeat in many typeface designs; the workstation's programs allow the lettering artist to copy and mirror parts of one character and apply them to others, thus ensuring the consistency of shapes in a typeface. Electronic rulers are used to check and/or define an alphabet's stem widths, italic angle, cap height, x-height, figure height, and so forth. Several characters can be displayed side by side to adjust side bearings. Additional electronic aids such as scaling and rotating character parts have resulted in a rapid average production rate of 20 minutes per character. When the 120 characters of a typical font are completed, they are copied onto large rolls of paper and checked for shape and fit.

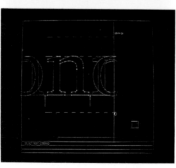

The characters' control points are listed on computer tapes and shipped to customers, companies that manufacture digital typesetters or imagesetters.

Digital Type Masters

How is the quality of typographic shapes affected by digital technology?

Digital typesetters can set type at resolutions high enough to ensure that individual dots are not discernible to the naked eye; but faster speeds are achieved when fewer dots need to be drawn.

Economical storage techniques allow a digital typesetter to set characters with precise curves at sizes below 4 points and well above ten inches from one master. But most typefaces are best represented by a different design for text sizes than for display sizes, and various cuts of a typeface should be available for different reproduction techniques.

▶When the 120 characters of a typical font are completed, they're checked for shape and fit.

Electronic techniques can produce the typeface alterations by condensing, expanding, slanting, shading, and warping characters, as well as combining characteristics of one typeface with another to produce a third. The results are usually available as an option, but a true italic is occasionally substituted by a slanted roman.

Specific spacing for kerning requirements can be stored for character pairs, but as individual cases increase, typesetting speed decreases.

New techniques in the production of digital type deserve scrutiny. Technology has both improved and diminished the quality of typographic forms. Graphic designers have direct communication with the owners of digital typesetting equipment and can, through them, express concerns, recommendations, and approval to manufacturers of digital type and typesetting equipment.

◆ Update: Software for creating digital type masters, though not as sophisticated as Bitstream's, is now available to independent type designers. See chapter 35, "Commission a Typeface."

3

Pointing Devices

Computer companies have put a

lot of work into making their computers easy to use: no more studying complex codes and typing them on imposing keyboards. From
now on, point. Point to things on the screen, like the symbol for a
paintbrush. Then point to the area where you want to begin painting. Press a button and electronic ink starts to flow. Point to an
eraser and clean up your mistakes.

You point with a *mouse,* a small box that fits comfortably under
your hand. As you move the mouse along the desk, a pointing symbol (*cursor*) moves correspondingly across the screen. Move the mouse
left, the cursor moves left. Move it slowly, the cursor moves slowly.
The mouse is based on the principle of eye/hand coordination, and

▶A mouse.

if you're skeptical about its intuitive ease of use, think about turning the steering wheel of a car as
you drive. It's second nature.

There are many other pointing
devices besides mice. Efforts to
provide *user-friendly interaction* have

Pointing Devices

resulted in a wide variety of shapes and sizes. One of the more widely used pointing devices in the graphic arts market is the combination of the stylus and tablet. It's a good example of how pointing devices work.

►A stylus and tablet.

A tablet is a smooth surface over a very fine grid. It's like electronic graph paper. Each intersection of grid lines is a *coordinate point*. Every point is represented by a pair of horizontal and vertical numbers to indicate its location. As you move the tip of the stylus across the tablet, the *x* (horizontal) and *y* (vertical) numbers of each coordinate point it contacts are sent to the computer. The computer instantaneously moves the cursor on the screen so that its *x,y* location corresponds to the *x,y* location of the stylus on the tablet's grid.

The stylus (or any pointing device) is used to select a graphic element such as headline type or a rule, and to select a menu command for that element, for example, "move," "copy," or "rotate." Place the cursor on the item, then press down and release the tip of the stylus. You've made a selection. To draw, keep pressing down while moving the stylus.

A digitizing puck often replaces a stylus when the job calls for great accuracy, as in plotting points along graphs, blueprints, maps, or artwork of typefaces to create digital character masters for digital type (see chapter 2, "Digital Type Masters"). A tablet typically has an accuracy of one-thousandth of an inch. The artwork is taped onto the tablet, and the puck is carefully placed over the points to be entered. A button on the puck is pressed to enter a point. A puck has cross hairs in flat glass,

►A digitizing puck.

Design and Technology

sometimes a magnifying glass for more precise placement. As the points of the artwork are entered, they appear on the screen.

▶A trackball.

A *trackball* is a ball bearing inside a box or a keyboard. Only the top of the ball is exposed. As you rotate the ball, sensors inside the box keep track of the number and direction of rotations. The cursor or selected item on the screen travels in whatever direction you spin the ball. The mouse is an upside-down trackball–the ball is underneath the box. Instead of moving your hand over the ball, you are moving the ball over the desk.

There are pointing devices that are more direct. While some computer companies say "point," others say "touch." The frame around a *position-sensitive screen* has light-emitting diodes along the bottom and the right, as well as receptors along the top and left that work like electronic eyes. When you point to the screen, your finger breaks the field of crisscrossing light beams. The x,y number for that coordinate point is registered.

▶A position-
sensitive
screen.

Pointing Devices

►A touch-
sensitive
screen.

Touch-sensitive screens, on the other hand, react to the pressure of
your finger. These screens are used in MIT's "movie manuals," in
which touching a picture activates an explanation of, for example,
how to fix an engine. Some screens respond to variable pressure—press
harder and you get a bigger blob of paint.

Like any tool, the choice of a pointing device depends on its availa-
bility, cost, ease of use, precision, and the type of work you have to
perform. The pointing device that seems awkward at first may turn
out to be the most preferable. For example, when you use a mouse
on a desk, or a stylus on a tablet, your drawing is on a separate
surface, the screen. Your work is not obstructed by a tool or by
your hand. The cursor represents the tip of the tool, and it can be
as small and precise as the resolution of the screen allows.

Pointing devices are an important factor in making computers
a natural part of graphic design. Experimental work that combines
sophisticated software with pointing devices hints of much more
to come. Imagine designing a page with an electronic cuff link on
your sleeve. Sit way back in your chair and point to an illustration
on the page (screen). Speak slowly, so the computer can understand you. "Put that" (then point to a location on the screen) "there."

Captured
Keystrokes

A large percentage of your typesetting bill is the cost of the time that the typesetting operator spends on your job. It's not the actual setting of type that is so expensive; that part is automated. It's the preparation of the text for the typesetting machine that is time-consuming. The three major areas that occupy an operator's time are 1) keyboarding the text; 2) entering typographic instructions into the typesetting machine; and 3) proofing. Because many designers' clients are avid users of word processors, much of this work can be accomplished outside the type shop, sometimes cutting the typesetting bill in half.

What are captured keystrokes?

Frequently the manuscript copy that a client delivers to a design studio has been typed on a word processor. All of the copy is in the form of captured keystrokes; the word processor records—captures—each character. The text can be played back to reappear on the word processor's screen for additions, corrections, and any other editing. Or the text can be sent to an electronic typewriter which, like any typewriter, prints the characters on paper.

Captured Keystrokes

The text is recorded on a *floppy disk,* a plastic disk that looks like a 45 rpm record with a thin protective jacket. The disk can be removed and inserted back into the word processor at any time to edit or print the text.

That same floppy disk can be played back on the equipment at the type shop. By receiving the manuscript as captured keystrokes, the operator can eliminate the step of rekeyboarding the same text.

Because the operator is not typing the manuscript, editorial proofreading at the type shop is also eliminated. Conventionally, when the operator types the manuscript copy at the typesetting machine, new errors are often introduced. By feeding the actual keystrokes into the typesetter, the copy is exactly the same as it was on the client's word processor. All editorial responsibility now lies with the client.

Capturing the keystrokes of manuscript text itself does not involve any typographic specifications, and the designer still marks up the *hard* (paper) *copy.* However, the word processor can be further utilized when the designer, type shop, and client collaborate to include typographic information with the manuscript.

In Boston, the design studio Sametz Blackstone Associates and several of its clients, along with Monotype Composition Company, routinely make use of word processors as an integral part of typesetting. The following steps of a typical job illustrate the process of sending a floppy disk of captured keystrokes and typographic information to the type shop.

❶ Using the conventional manner of specing type, the designer has sample pages typeset, then sends them to the client for approval.

❷ When the sample pages are approved, the designer has a sample typeset of every typographic element that will be in that job, again in the conventional manner. For each variation, the type shop designates a specific mnemonic code, a *format call,* for each element.

A format call is an abbreviation that represents a lengthy set of specifications. In this particular job, ;r is short for roman, 10/12 Bodoni x 17 picas, flush left ragged right. The typesetting machine

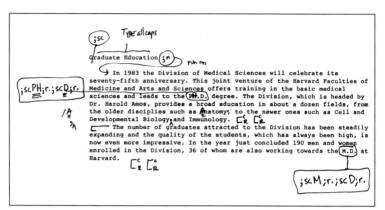

is programmed (instructed) to set all text following ;r to those specifications. All text is set to those specs until the machine encounters another instruction, such as ;sc, which represents a different set of specifications, this time for small caps.

❸ The designer then marks up the manuscript with these codes and returns it to the client. The client's word processing operator enters these codes on the word processor with the rest of the manuscript. Just as the manuscript text is recorded on a floppy disk, so are the format calls. Because the text and the format calls are not rekeyboarded at the type shop, the word processing operator must make sure that he or she has included all necessary text and codes.

```
G;scRADUATE EDUCATION;nIn 1983 the Division of Medical Sciences will
celebrate its seventy-fifth anniversary. This joint venture of the
Harvard Faculties of Medicine and Arts and Sciences offers training in
the basic medical sciences and leads to the ;scPH;r.;scD;r. degree. The
Division, which is headed by Dr. Harold Amos, provides a broad education
in about a dozen fields, from the older disciplines such as Anatomy, to
the newer ones such as Cell and Developmental Biology and Immunology.

The number of graduates attracted to the Division has been steadily
expanding and the quality of the students, which has always been high, is
now even more impressive. In the year just concluded 190 men and women
enrolled in the Division, 36 of whom are also working towards the
;scM;r.;scD;r. at Harvard.
```

❹ The client sends the disk (and a hard-copy version as backup) to the designer, or directly to the type shop. When the disk arrives at the type shop, a skilled operator must set up a *translation table.* To a designer, the format call ;r is an abbreviation for 10/12 Bodoni roman. To the typesetting machine, it is an abbreviation for a much longer and more complex code that the machine understands. The translation table tells the typesetting machine that every time it encounters a ;r in the manuscript, it should carry out the long, complex set of machine instructions that are associated with ;r. When the machine encounters ;sc, it carries out a different set of instructions.

❺ The type shop then sends the typeset galleys back to the designer and a copy of the galleys, with the disk, to the client. Turnaround time is short: 12 galleys of type overnight, 70 galleys in 48 hours. The galleys are pasted up in the conventional manner. If there are extensive changes, they are made on the client's word processor, and the disk is sent back to the type-setter. Sametz Blackstone has noticed a marked decrease in corrections and/or AAs.

> GRADUATE EDUCATION In 1983 the Division of Medical Sciences will celebrate its seventy-fifth anniversary. This joint venture of the Harvard Faculties of Medicine and Arts and Sciences offers training in the basic medical sciences and leads to the PH.D. degree. The Division, which is headed by Dr. Harold Amos, provides a broad education in about a dozen fields, from the older disciplines such as Anatomy, to the newer ones such as Cell and Developmental Biology, and Immunology.
>
> The number of graduates attracted to the Division has been steadily expanding and the quality of the students, which has always been high, is now even more impressive. In the year just concluded 190 men and women enrolled in the Division, 36 of whom are also working towards the M.D. at Harvard.

▶The type shop sends the typeset galleys back to the designer and a copy of the galleys, with the floppy disk, to the client.

Various type shops agree that including format calls with the word processor's captured keystrokes is economical only if the job is long and repetitive. It takes a skilled operator a long time to set up the translation tables, and if the job is short and has a lot of variety, it's easier for the operator to type the machine codes directly from reading the designer's conventionally marked-up manuscript. A 200-page college catalog, on the other hand, is very repetitive. The setup time is short compared to the time it would take to repeatedly type the machine language codes. And format calls can be used for any job that repeats a set of specifications, such as a monthly newsletter or magazine. As the repetition adds up, the savings accrue.

At Typographic House in Boston, about 25 percent of the customers send manuscript copy in the form of captured keystrokes, and of those customers, about 10 percent include format calls. Typesetting costs are cut by about 40 percent (depending on the length) for jobs that have text keystrokes only. If format calls are included, another 15 percent might be saved.

Typographic House recently purchased a *preview screen,* a video display terminal that shows a simulation of the text in the point size, leading, style, column width, and so forth that will be typeset. It is much easier for the typesetting operator to catch errors on this preview screen than on a regular video display terminal, where the long codes are difficult to distinguish from the manuscript text. And it is much more economical to catch errors before the job is typeset on expensive film or RC paper.

Most type shops have a wealth of information and suggestions, and it is their goal and responsibility to keep designers informed and productive. It's no surprise to Typographic House that many designers would like to have the advantage of a preview of their job before it is typeset. Material is delivered from place to place on floppy disks and played back on a variety of machines, from word processors to typesetters to preview screens. (Translations are necessary, but standards are emerging.) The simulation of a typeset page could be stored on a floppy disk and displayed on a preview screen at a design studio.

As computer workstations become less expensive and more user-friendly, designers will have more than preview screens; we'll also be able to specify type on our own equipment. Eventually, this will lead to the elimination of the type shop as we know it. As a result, we'll have more control, but also more responsibility.

◆ Update: Using personal computers and page layout software, many designers have become their own typesetters. But the quality and expertise expected from a good type shop has yet to be replaced.

Trade Shows

Wandering through your first graphic arts trade show is like traveling in a foreign country; it's strange and overwhelming, and you feel as if you can't possibly take it all in. But when you get home you realize how much insight you've gained.

A trade show is the best way to get an overview of the latest graphic arts technology. These shows are for exposure: Exhibitors can display new equipment to hundreds of potential customers, and attendees can do extensive comparative shopping, all within a few days. A trade show is one of the few places that designers can get a close look at a lot of new and expensive equipment.

The most visually exciting examples of new technology are the workstations for assembling pages. I went to a trade show recently where there were more than 20 companies—some well established, some start-up—exhibiting "pagination (page layout) video terminal systems." Each company's workstation has a video screen showing type and illustrations. You can manipulate these elements interactively, that is, specify actions, such as moving a block of text or changing a point size, and see the results immediately.

These companies are focusing on prepress tasks that are labor-intensive. They're developing computer-aided methods for specifying type, sizing and cropping line art and photographs, making layouts, paginating, proofing, editing, correcting, pasting up, airbrushing, masking, stripping, and so on. Each company makes broad claims. How can you qualify the differences between the workstations? Which differences are superficial and which are profound?

The best way to understand this equipment is through your own experience. These workstations are being developed for the production of printed material.

As I went from booth to booth, watching rehearsed demonstrations and collecting pounds of literature, I considered each product's application. The page makeup workstations fell into three categories: first, technical publishing (long documents); second, black-and-white ads (or complicated single pages); and third, four-color ads (or complicated single pages).

Workstations for technical publishing are designed to handle large amounts of text. They emphasize pagination; a long manuscript automatically flows into a specified grid, jumps over illustrations, and breaks at the end of a column, page, or chapter, with no orphans or widows. Remove an illustration or add a paragraph and the text automatically reflows, incorporating all changes. But there are only a few type styles on the screen, called generic fonts, that represent the larger assortment on the typesetter—if there is an interface to a typesetter.

Black-and-white ad layout (single-page layout) terminals feature easy manipulation of individual elements. You can change a text block's typeface, point size, rotation, and column width, or create decorative borders, line art, reverses, and overlaps. But these workstations are inefficient at processing large amounts of text.

The color workstation demonstrations are fascinating: The operator airbrushes away a pair of glasses and changes skin tones. The typefaces are true and the pictures will be made into accurate four-color separations. But the text is not handled with the interactive ease and speed of the black-and-white systems.

Look at each workstation in the context of the big picture. Does it connect to the necessary word processor, image scanner, typesetter, imagesetter, or proof printer? Some companies are addressing disparate tasks in one big workstation. Are they considering the different professional experience necessary for each task?

Finally, does the product really exist? Because the planning of a trade show starts a year and a half in advance, a company has to make a commitment to exhibit long before it has a completed product. Typically the company doesn't quite meet the deadline. The equipment is still in prototype form, and the technical staff is on hand to fix whatever breaks. It reminds me of the Wizard of Oz: "Pay no attention to the man behind the curtain."

It helps to do some research before you go to a trade show. Telephone the organizers to find out exactly what the show is covering, and which companies will be exhibiting. Request preview material so that you can read about who's showing what.

Don't worry if all you've seen seems a blur. A week or so after you get home from a trade show, pick up a trade magazine that's covered the show. Combine its analysis with your own recollections. The next time you spec type or paste up a mechanical, you'll realize how much insight you've gained.

◆ Update: There are hundreds of computer graphics trade shows every year of interest to graphic designers. See appendix A.

6

Resolution

When we first saw galleys from a digital typesetter, all of us in the design department were disappointed. Optima looked awful, Bodoni worse. We had heard that this kind of technology produced "jaggies," stairsteps along the edge of a character, so all of us had our loupes out looking for the culprit. We were sure that the lack of quality had something to do with the typesetter's *resolution.*

We were already familiar with the subject of resolution. It's an important factor in reproducing artwork. When you decide to use a 200-line halftone screen, you're choosing a resolution. When you select a particular photographic paper or film, you're choosing a resolution. You choose the amount of precision that best suits your artwork.

How is resolution measured?

A digital typesetter's resolution is described by the number of dots per vertical inch. Each character is made up of many slightly overlapping, same-sized dots. On a thousand-dot-per-inch typesetter, a character that's exactly one inch tall has 1,000 dots from top to bottom. (The horizontal number is usually the same, so a typesetter with a resolution of 1,000 dots per inch would have 1,000,000 dots per square inch.) With a resolution that high, it's nearly impossible to perceive the individual dots with the naked

Resolution

eye. Some digital typesetters have a resolution of over 5,000 dots per inch. On the other end of the scale, computer printers typically have fewer than 150 dots per inch.

In the same way, the resolution of a computer graphics workstation is described by the number of horizontal and vertical *pixels* (picture elements or dots) on its video screen. Screens that have fewer than 200 pixels in each direction are considered low resolution. High-resolution screens have over 1,000 pixels in each direction. Just as the resolution of a halftone screen affects the precision of a photograph, the resolution of the video screen affects the precision of an image.

Resolution can also refer to the number of colors that an individual pixel can be. Some computer graphic workstations can show only eight colors; others can show literally millions. In offset printing, the wide variety of colors is achieved by mixing different combinations of inks with varying amounts (parts) of each. On a video screen, the color of a pixel is determined by a combination of red, green, and/or blue light, with varying intensities of each. Even white, black, and shades of gray are colors: mixtures of red, green, and blue.

In print or video, if the horizontal and vertical resolution is quite low, it's possible to see "jaggies." Adding color values visually smooths out those edges. Think of a diagonal line made of black blocks. The corners are very obvious. Now think of a gray block tucked in each corner. On video screens, the smoothing effect is surprisingly successful, even though it seems paradoxical: smoother shapes from fuzzier edges. The first illustration shows the same type as the second. The

►These characters are made up only of black-and-white pixels.

►The same characters are made up of pixels that are black, white, and two levels of gray.

only difference is that the characters in the first are made of black-and-white pixels only; in the second they are black, white, and two levels of gray. You could think of them as continuous tone characters.

Why is higher resolution more expensive?

In computer graphics, the higher the resolution, the more dots the computer has to remember. Characters on a digital typesetter are "drawn" by a fine beam of light. The beam is instructed by the typesetter's computer to turn on and off as it traverses light-sensitive paper, exposing dots that make up the typographic shapes. Even with software shortcuts, 1,000,000 dots per square inch is a lot to keep track of, and computer memory costs money.

The computer sends instructions to "light up" pixels to construct a given shape on a video screen. If the workstation has color, the computer has to include color instructions for each pixel. Imagine a screen that has 1,000,000 pixels, with 1,000,000 possible colors for each pixel. ...

Speed is another important cost factor. Not only does the computer have to remember which dots are "on" and which are "off," it has to send those on/off instructions to each dot at a very high speed.

An interactive workstation—one with which a designer can move and manipulate images on the video screen—has the additional factor of change. Every time you electronically move, shrink, rotate, or paint an image on the screen, the computer sends new instructions to each pixel (see chapter 3, "Pointing Devices"). To keep up with your movements, the computer must send thousands of instructions within fractions of a second.

Basically, cost depends on the amount of dots, colors, and speed. The higher the numbers, the higher the cost.

Does quantity produce quality?

Don't assume that high resolution is the answer to all problems. It's important to remember that in any medium, higher resolution will not make a bad image good. We searched the galleys of

Optima and Bodoni in vain for those jaggies; the poor quality had nothing to do with resolution. The typesetting manufacturer used poorly drawn original artwork to make the digital type. We complained to the manufacturer, who finally hired people with the proper design expertise to re-create the digital alphabets. The next galleys—with the same resolution—were much better.

What is the best resolution?

Design jobs have many stages, and each stage requires a different amount of resolution and speed. Some jobs require comps that are nearly printed pieces, while others can have roughs that are barely legible. When you purchase, rent, or use computer graphic equipment, your choices will depend on familiar questions: How fast? How good? How much?

7

The Electronic Workflow

I met a woman who told me, "I'm saving the columns you've written; I'm not ready to read them yet." She explained that she was eager to learn, but didn't understand how each piece of technology related to her everyday workflow. This made me think about the context of all these new devices. One hears about word processors, scanners, high-speed printers, page layout terminals, imagesetters. ... How can these "boxes" be used to collect raw materials, design a comp, and make a mechanical?

Take an example of a small black-and-white brochure. You already know the traditional tools, materials, and procedures required to produce a finished mechanical from a typewritten manuscript and some 8 x 10 photographs. How would you create that brochure using "state-of-the-art" technology?

COLLECT RAW MATERIALS

The copywriter composes the text on a word processor. If you've ever used one, you know how much easier it is to make changes or correct typos than with a typewriter. The "raw text" is electronically transferred, by a cable, from the word processor to the page layout terminal. If the two pieces of equipment are not in the same building, the text is transferred by *modem*—a device hooked up to a telephone—or delivered on a floppy disk. The raw manuscript is stored at the page layout terminal, where it waits for specifications.

Photographs are scanned—translated into black-and-white dots much like a halftone screen—with an *input scanner* or *digitizing camera.* The digitized photographs are transmitted to the page layout terminal, where they will be sized, cropped, and positioned.

PRODUCE A COMP

Traditionally, you might use press type for headlines, send some text out to typeset sample body copy, and order stats to create the comp for the brochure. With a page layout terminal, those tools, services, and graphic elements are available in-house. By selecting from a *menu,* you can copy, scale, reverse, stretch, crop, or combine elements.

Remember the raw copy? Typeset the text on the screen by selecting a typeface, point size, leading, and measure from another menu. If it's too big, make it smaller. Or change the typeface. Or use a different face for each word. The results of your specifications for each design element appear on the screen within seconds. If you think of a better headline, type it on the keyboard; it appears immediately, for your decision on face, size, and letterspacing to make it absolutely perfect.

Consider what's traditionally required to test design alternatives. Because of the expense, both in time and money, it's unlikely that you would produce five or six different trials of typefaces and point sizes, let alone percentage screens or photographic manipulations. With this interactive technology, you can make your ideas visible as they come to mind, and make your final decisions in one work session.

By pointing to another menu option, the pages of the brochure are transmitted to the *proof printer,* and a replica of what you created on the screen is copied onto paper. You can make a copy of the screen at any time, producing comps of numerous design variations.

MAKE THE MECHANICAL

At the page layout terminal, when you choose the specifications and placement for each element of your comp, you are simultaneously creating your mechanical. The type is set, the photographs are cropped and sized, the stats are made, and the mechanical is pasted up. The elements that you see on the screen are representations of the same elements stored at a much higher resolution in the computer.

The high-resolution version of the brochure pages is transmitted to the imagesetter, which sets images as well as type on film or repro paper (see chapter 1, "Imagesetters"). The entire mechanical is set. Your job is finished.

◆ Update: In 1985, the combination of the Macintosh, the LaserWriter, and PageMaker began to make the electronic workflow a reality for designers. See chapter 12, "Time to Buy?"

If the copywriter calls with emergency text changes, bring your finished page back to the screen of the page makeup terminal. Make the necessary corrections at the keyboard, removing or inserting characters. The text automatically recomposes to accommodate the changes. Transmit the corrected page to the imagesetter, and you will have your new mechanical.

Some of the pieces of equipment described in the above scenario are still in development labs, others are in production facilities, but few are in graphic design studios. For the graphic designer, the ability to test alternatives, consolidate tasks, eliminate pasteup, and easily make corrections can mean a more efficient, and therefore more profitable, workflow.

Which pieces are you ready for?

8

Many Tools, One Box

I glanced at the top of the screen: 19:32:02. It had been a long day. I was using a new word processor, and felt frustrated with its myriad of obscure codes. I pressed the keys *escape, k, s,* and *print,* and headed for the coffee machine.

As I walked by one of the studios, I peeked in the door. A designer was working on a comp for an ad. He sat at a workstation: a streamlined desk with a color video screen, a keyboard, and a mouse. To his left was a video camera on a copy stand; to his right was a color proof printer and a slide recorder.

The screen displayed a white page with a headline in Garamond. I watched the designer as he continued to design the ad, studying his movements so that I could understand how the system worked. He slid the mouse across the desk, and a pointer moved across the screen. He pressed a button on the mouse, and the pointer turned into a small, empty rectangle. As he moved the mouse, the rectangle grew. He pressed the button again, and the rectangle was replaced by a full-color photograph, shocking in its contrast to the stark black-and-white page. He pressed a different button; as though changing channels, the page disappeared and the screen displayed

► The designer created the image with the tools of the workstation, including a mouse, a video camera, and a keyboard.

a menu of choices, ranging from shapes and tools to a palette of smoothly blended colors. He made his selections, switched back to the page, and began to paint with a bright yellow rectangular "brush."

With a series of menu selections, he altered the image by adding type, airbrushing, and cutting out pieces of the picture to rotate, mirror, scale, and layer. As I watched the comp take shape, I realized that he was employing the tools and services of a well-equipped design and photography studio without moving from his chair.

Before long I was as absorbed as he was. I forgot about the menu, the mouse, how the system worked. My attention was held by the rapidity of change and the clarity of elements so familiar to my trade—typefaces, photographs, and color. I was seeing graphic design as a performing art.

An insistent beep from the other room broke the spell; the word processor's printer had finished printing out my text.

I paced as I read, and nearly tripped over a heavy extension cord. Someone was carrying around a video camera, pointing it out the window at the skyline, the water, the traffic. I followed the cord from the camera to another studio, where there was a workstation identical to the one I'd seen in the first studio. Instead of using the camera to transmit an existing photograph to the screen, the photographer had removed the camera from the copy stand for some live material. Cars were moving across the workstation's screen, and another designer was studying the images, now and then pressing a button to "freeze" and save moments. One frozen picture was of me, tripping over the extension cord!

This photographer/designer team continued to freeze images. I

Many Tools, One Box

watched for a few minutes, witnessing a dialogue of subtle progressions. They finished when the sun went down.

Not at all ready to *escape, k, retrieve,* and *edit,* I wandered back to the first studio. The ad looked quite different. He had removed some type, moved everything down so that the headline really stood out, and changed the size of the photograph. His new design was twice as powerful.

He leaned back and reviewed his final comp. I heard a click—he had pressed a foot pedal. With that, the image on the screen was transmitted to the slide recorder, and ninety seconds later he had a slide of his comp. He had saved a few variations, making a slide of each, and he put them all in a slide tray.

He typed a memo to his boss on an electric typewriter, and I asked him why he didn't use the word processor. "I wish I could," he said, "but it's too complicated. I simply don't have the time to learn." I looked at the workstation, the ultimate in high technology. This designer had just produced a full-color comp, complete with typography, photography, and hand-painted imagery. The workstation's computer had just moved millions of bits, exercised thousands of algorithms, performed computational acrobatics the likes of which no word processor has ever seen.

As he put on his coat, I glanced at the screen of the word processor: 20:38:46. I decided to follow his lead.

Escape, k, s, exit.

9

Increasing Idea Time

The Macmillan Press, Ltd., in Great

Britain publishes a series of music dictionaries; the next volume to be produced in the series is the *Dictionary of American Music.* Alyn Shipton, the music publisher at Macmillan, wanted to ensure an appropriately and thoroughly American package for the book, so he asked Robert Updegraff, the company's chief London designer, to recommend an American to design the case.

On Robert's recommendation, Alyn contacted Nathan Felde. Alyn's letter to Nathan served as both an introduction and a design brief. The brief was not unusual; it was partly specific, partly loose. "The style for the spine ... should relate in colour, style, typeface and capitalization to the [other Grove publications], but not in *every* one of these factors.... This should look as *American* as possible.... The end result should be tasteful and up-market, and right for academic libraries and musicologists." He included an existing cover with the brief.

Robert had suggested Nathan for good reason. Nathan's design process is particularly well suited to the speed, versatility, and flexibility that Alyn needed.

Nathan sat down with the brief at his workstation. The color video screen serves as a drawing board; in addition, it has a set of menu selections that include a wide range of tools, type, shapes, color, and so forth. Sliding the mouse across the desk moves a pointer across the screen. Everything on the screen is accessible by pointing.

Nathan placed the cover of an existing dictionary on the video camera's copy stand and transmitted the image to the screen to use as a basis for his design. He copied the spine a few times to make a full bookshelf, and by indicating a small rectangular area of the spine, he made a "book-cloth brush" and painted out the typography on the copied spines. He typed the new title in Helvetica, wrapping letters along a curve. He selected another color and flooded it over the spine; it neatly surrounded the type. He tried a few more typefaces, colors, textures, and layouts. He experimented with changes freely, because he could restore earlier versions at any time.

Within an hour and a half, he had full-color, actual-type thumbnails. He transmitted the images on the screen to a film recorder, sent the film out for processing, and was looking at slides two hours later. Because the first part of the project had been completed so quickly, he had the luxury of letting his ideas "cook" for a few days, instead of having to rush them off with the next courier. He put them in a drawer and turned to other work.

Over the next two days he made slight adjustments, testing them against his initial conclusions. He decided to send his first thumbnails anyway, but was pleased that he'd had those few days of leeway. The slides arrived in London the next day.

What typically goes through a designer's mind when presenting a comp? "How much *additional* work—stats, typesetting, materials, board work—must I do if my client requests changes?" There's a natural tendency to protect the heavy investment of time and materials that you've already made.

Nathan's conversation with Alyn had a rather different flavor. Because he knew that minimal time and money would be spent between receiving Alyn's feedback, making the changes, and producing a new version, he could concentrate on the most important aspect of the designer/client relationship: the exchange of ideas. In fact, his first question to Alyn was "What would you like to change?"

▶By scanning, duplicating, and painting over the spine of the existing dictionary, Nathan Felde used his workstation to create a bookshelf of design options. This is the second (final) comp.

They decided to take one idea much further and explore another, new alternative. As a follow-up to their phone call, Alyn sent a telex to Nathan asking when he could have revised visuals. That was Thursday. On Tuesday the new slides were in London. Cromalins were made (to size) for marketing meetings. There was very little discussion at that point, and Alyn telexed the choices and modifications to be incorporated when typesetting the final mechanical.

At the end of the week Alyn had to be in Boston, so he stopped by Nathan's office to see the "new tools" that had produced the comps. Ironically, Nathan was in Europe, and their transatlantic relationship was maintained. Alyn got a demonstration of how that variety of visuals was produced in so short a time, and he quickly understood the flexibility that these tools afforded. Later I asked Alyn if he had been influenced by the technology during the project. He said, "The job was all done by the time I realized how simple it was."

Ideas are as important to your client as they are to you. By cutting way down on materials, labor, and turnaround time, these tools reduce production time and increase idea time. And that encourages a more creative dialogue between designer and client.

Quick Corrections

Jim taped down the tracing paper over the last board and telephoned the printer.

"Can you come by and pick up the mechanicals?"

"Sure, right after lunch."

Jim collected the pieces of the job—the mechanicals plus the slides with approved Cromalins and four-color separations—and filled out a list of instructions. Just as he was writing the printer's name and address on a large manila envelope, his extension buzzed. He picked up the phone: It was his client.

"Jim, I know this is late notice, but we just have to change a few words in one paragraph."

Jim said, "No problem," copied down the new sentence, and hung up the phone.

Oh, well. This happens to designers all the time; it's nothing to worry about.

He looked at the mechanical for that spread. It had a couple of headlines, a huge ampersand, two paragraphs of justified type, one of which ran around the side of the ampersand, and two numbered black rectangles to indicate where to drop in the color pictures.

Jim ripped up the mechanical and tossed it into the wastebasket.

He swiveled his chair around to face a black-and-white monitor, a keyboard, and a mouse. By sliding the mouse along the table, he moved a pointer on the screen to a numbered list of the spreads for the brochure. He clicked a button on the mouse and selected the number for the double-page spread he had to correct. Within a few seconds the spread appeared, complete with all the elements—headlines, paragraphs, ampersand, black rectangles, and crop marks.

Jim had made the brochure mechanicals at this page design terminal, creating the typographic elements, laying them out on the screen, then transmitting the completed spreads to a typesetting machine.

To make the correction that his client requested, he simply continued working in the same manner. He selected the incorrect sentence and then selected the word *remove* from a menu. The paragraph disappeared and then immediately reappeared without the incorrect sentence, rejustified.

Then Jim typed the new sentence into the paragraph. As he typed, the new words appeared in the same typeface, point size, and measure as the rest of the paragraph, still wrapping around the side of the ampersand. With the new sentence, the paragraph was a line shorter, and Jim had liked the way it had filled the space before. He changed the leading by adding one point. That looked too open, so he changed it back.

He decided to move the whole paragraph down. Now the runaround was the wrong shape, so he redrew the outline around the paragraph, and the words flowed into the new shape.

While he was at it, Jim selected one of the black rectangles that indicated the placement of a picture and moved it horizontally, just a hair closer to the paragraph of text.

Satisfied now with the way everything looked, Jim made another selection from the menu and sent the double-page spread to the typesetting machine down the hall. Because all the elements on the pages are transmitted electronically, if Jim's studio didn't have a typesetter he could have transmitted the mechanical over the telephone to a type shop, if the shop had the same kind of typesetter.

He waited a few minutes, then walked to the typesetter. He lifted the light-tight cassette out of the machine, and inserted it into a film-and-paper processor.

Just as the repro paper came out of the processor, the printer arrived. Jim checked to make sure that everything was in place: the headlines, ampersand, corrected copy, numbered black rectangles, and crop marks. He taped the mechanical to a piece of cardboard so that it wouldn't crease, covered it with tracing paper, and slid it into the envelope that had the other boards, slides, Cromalins, separations, and instruction sheet. He taped the envelope closed and handed it to the printer.

Finally. Now Jim could get some lunch.

♦ Update: What happens when your clients have the equipment to make their own corrections? See chapter 22, "Keeping Up with Your Clients."

11

. . . .

Greetings from Design

The mechanicals for *Design Source,* a directory of creative services in New England, were nearly finished, except for the section title pages. As a matter of fact, those hadn't been designed yet. George Turnbull, the publisher, described the job to Mary Anne Lloyd: 12 full-color pages using the theme of old postcards.

They sketched out a format. Each page would have a black-and-white collage of old postcard pictures for the background, with a four-color postcard, designed by Mary Anne, set in the background at an angle. Each color postcard would have the title of the section that it introduces: Marketing, Photo, Film, Design, Paper, and so forth.

George sent over 12 envelopes, each of which contained a batch of old postcards, a description of the theme of each subject, and a black-and-white hand-lettered title.

Mary Anne piled the envelopes on the floor next to the media and design workstation. She opened the first envelope and arranged the cards onto the video camera's copy stand. By pressing a button on the puck, she scanned the image in black and white, and it

Greetings from Design

▶The workstation's video camera captures three-dimensional objects as well as flat images, so Mary Anne Lloyd collected props to scan.

appeared simultaneously on the video screen. After completing the background arrangement and manipulation, she pressed another button and saved the image in the computer's storage. The 12 title page backgrounds were finished in a couple of hours.

Then she brought out a box of props that she'd gathered to use in the color postcards. The video camera can capture three-dimensional objects as well as flat artwork, so Mary Anne had collected

►Mary Anne used the title lettering as an electronic orthofilm mask, with the color pictures showing through.

magazine pictures, pieces of old wallpaper, chalk, Band-Aids, the top of a pineapple–things that related (sometimes obscurely) to each of the sections. Selecting from the workstation's menus of tools, brushes, shapes, colors, and type, she created the color postcards.

I asked Mary Anne to describe "Awards."

"First I scanned a magazine photograph of some clouds. Then I cut out a portion of the clouds and repeated it, in different sizes and proportions all over the screen. I smeared some of the edges.

"To make the title, I scanned the 'Awards' lettering he gave me. I used the lettering as a kind of electronic orthofilm mask so that the color pictures just show through the lettering with the pictures inside—on top of the clouds.

"I selected a script typeface and typed 'greetings from'; then I selected Helvetica and typed 'Design Source.' That's it. No, wait, I did one more thing: I smeared here and there to jazz it up."

Mary Anne transmitted the final designs of the black-and-white backgrounds and color postcards to the workstation's film recorder, then she sent the 35mm film to the photo lab for processing.

She delivered her "mechanicals" to George: 12 slides of black-and-white backgrounds, 12 slides of color postcards, and one slide of a color postcard dropped out of a black-and-white background to indicate correct positioning for the printer.

Mary Anne designed and produced 12 full-color pages, from roughs to final mechanicals, without buying any material or services other than 35mm film, film processing—and a pineapple.

12

Time to Buy?

Thanks to Hurricane Gloria, the attendees of the 1985 AIGA conference had extra time to give their own speeches to each other. Here's one that I got:

"The personal computer is the wok of the 1980s."

"What do you mean?" I asked.

"Do you own a wok?"

"Well, I bought one, but I only used it once. Now it's just collecting dust."

"Precisely!"

True, I purchased the wok because of its sudden popularity and implicit promises. It would make me a better, faster, healthier cook. Forty dollars, two unread cookbooks, and an unopened bottle of soy sauce later, my cooking habits remain unaltered.

He continued. "All these designers are eager to buy personal computers. Every time they open a newspaper, they see ads for a computer, software, and a printer for less than $4,000. Sure, that may be cheap for a piece of high technology. But do they *need* it?"

I saw his point. There is a lot of news about personal computers with software programs that aid in laying out pages, making charts and diagrams, fitting copy, editing text, and more, all without requiring a knowledge of programming or typesetting codes. The software packages are easy to learn and have features that, when used for the appropriate jobs, can save an impressive amount of time and money. Unfortunately, they are often solutions to some-one else's problems. If you don't purchase a tool based on your own needs, you may end up with a very expensive wok.

Our conversation ended when the conference chairman announced an open bar at a nearby hotel, but I was reminded of it when a friend told me this story:

"I pass a computer store every day on my way to work. Recently I've noticed some graphic design-related displays and advertise-ments, so I decided to investigate. I went inside, wandered around, collected brochures, and watched demonstrations. I got a head-ache and went home.

"Later that week, I was designing a direct mail piece for one of our steady clients, and as I flipped through half-used sheets of press type, I realized that I'd gone to the store with the wrong point of view. Instead of thinking about my own work, I was focusing on the tool.

"I went back to the store, armed with my rough sketches for the mail piece. I located a salesperson whose specialty was graph-ics, showed him my sketches, and said, I want to make this. What have you got? After a brief demonstration of a page layout pro-gram, I asked the salesperson for a few tips to get started, then asked him to leave me alone with the computer, but not to wander too far away, in case I got stuck.

"After 15 minutes of poking around and calling back the sales-person, I was ready to tackle some basics. I quickly began to see what was useful and what was limiting.

"I typed the headline copy and it appeared immediately on the screen in the typeface I'd chosen. I could easily change it to bold or italic. But there were only six typefaces from which to choose. I tried a range of point sizes, all the way up to 72 point. But above about 24 point, the letters became blocky, no longer a true repre-sentation of the typeface. I moved the type around on the screen; I could move it freely, or confine its movement to a specified grid. But the screen was smaller than 8½" x 11", and working at actual size I could see only a portion of the page.

Design and Technology

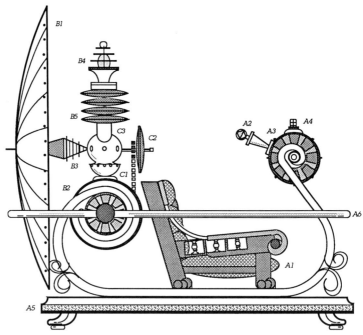

▶These illustrations were produced using an Apple Macintosh, an Apple PostScript LaserWriter, and various software programs.

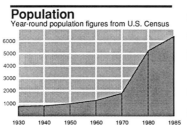

Population
Year-round population figures from U.S. Census

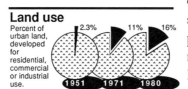

Land use
Percent of urban land, developed for residential, commercial or industrial use.

"I reduced the scale so that the whole page fit on the screen. That was comfortable. I like working on thumbnails.

"With the salesperson at my side (I was venturing into more complicated procedures), I defined a column format and type specs for body copy. I typed a few paragraphs, noting that if I was responsible for entering the text, I was also responsible for typos. I worked with the 'galleys' of body copy that I had just typed, 'cutting' a galley and moving the remainder to another column. It was a familiar way of working, with the added options of changing column width, typeface, point size, and leading within seconds.

Time to Buy?

"I needed to see something closer to the real thing: paper. I selected the menu option *print,* and the dot matrix printer began printing the page. Things were progressing well. I was impressed, and I think the salesperson was calculating his commission. Then I saw the page that came out of the printer.

" 'That looks dreadful! I wouldn't even use it for a comp.'

"I was about to give up the whole idea, but the salesperson had something else to show me. He reprinted the page on a new laser printer. It took a minute longer to print, but the type looked much better. The salesperson explained that, unlike the dot matrix printer, which produces a replica of the screen, the laser printer translates the type to a higher resolution of 300 dots per inch. Even though that's much lower than a typesetter [typically 1,000 dots per inch], it's adequate for a comp, and for some applications like newsletters, charts, and catalog sheets, it can be used for camera-ready artwork.

"So I continued to work, making variations and printing them on the laser printer, until the salesperson started to lock up. I asked him for a rundown on prices.

" 'The computer's $2,795. The software package that you were using is $495. I recommend extra memory, plus an external disk drive; that's $2,195 and $495, respectively. There are a lot of other software programs that you'd be interested in; they range from $20 to $500. The dot matrix printer is $595. All of that is retail, of course.'

"I pointed to the laser printer. 'How much is that?'

" 'Retail, $7,000.' "

My friend went back to her studio and discussed the subject with her colleagues. With the extra software and peripherals they were likely to need, the total price would easily exceed $13,000. Did they have enough work that would benefit from these tools? Was the quality too poor? Were the limitations too severe? Was $13,000 too much, or was it too little? Should they investigate a more expensive system that would cover a wider range of their work? Should they consider sharing the equipment with another design studio?

Weeks later, my friend is still visiting computer stores and reading newspaper ads, but with a different purpose: She's shopping for the best price. She may have found a Christmas bargain, at 20 percent off retail.

Speaking of Christmas, I wonder if there's anyone who could use a wok. . . .

Type Design

John brings a pot of his usual syrup-strength coffee into his living room/office. Steven has fired up the computer, and he gives me a demo of their latest software. It's fast and neat; the ease with which you can make and move and change text and shapes on the screen is fantastic. But their typeface is, frankly, ugly. As my friends argue the merits of one programming language over another, my mind wanders to Matthew Carter's slide presentation about the effect of technology on letterforms, and I recall his optimistic comment:

"Type is pretty adaptable, and when technology does show through, it's usually just briefly."

Matthew began his presentation by noting how fortunate he is to be among those who started working with type in the 1950s, the last generation to make type by all methods: hot metal, photocomposition, and digital technology. He illustrated the point by launching into a verbal array of the manufacturing processes:

"You cut it, cast it, draw it, pantograph it, frisket it, scan it, quantize it, generate it, digitize it, spline it, encode it, rasterize it, pixelate it, half-bit it, Cam it, Abe it, Fed it, Metafont it, toolbox it, plaid it, grayscale it, laserwrite it" … deep breath … "You try to design it, you try to read it."

Matthew encounters new limitations each time he creates a typeface for another phase of technology. He showed a study of the

►Helvetica Ultra Compressed, Helvetica Extra Compressed, and Helvetica Compressed, designed for Linofilm.

Helvetica Compressed Series he designed for Linofilm.

"We wanted to make a family of compressed sans serifs. The first job was to see how many different degrees of 'compressed-ness' were possible. In a compressed sans serif series, the stem weights of the single-, double-, and triple-stem characters (*i, n, m*) have to match and also fit into a regular progression of units. The counters and the space between the letters must be the same apparent width: a kind of picket fence rhythm. The oblique and round characters have to conform. With the Linofilm spacing system, the narrowest width was 4 units, the widest 18. We saw that there were only three possible 1-2-3 progressions that could be used between 4 and 18. If we'd had a 54-unit system (which came later, with the VIP), we would have had much more flexibility in choosing stem weights."

I've seen those faces so many times, never aware of the strict limitations that have been imposed on their design. That was the continuing theme of the presentation: Technology has surprisingly little effect on letters if the designer makes good, readable typefaces, and does a capable job of "flattering" less-than-perfect technology. As Matthew said, "When someone reads a bad typeface, he's not going to say, 'Poor fellow, he had an 18-unit Linofilm spacing system to deal with.'"

Although the Linofilm's photocomposition technology offered little benefit beyond hot metal for a compressed sans serif, especially with an 18-unit straitjacket, it gave Matthew the freedom to design Snell Roundhand. Charles Snell's late-17th-century accountant's script was virtually impossible in hot metal.

Photocomposition freed characters from their metallic constraints,

allowing ascenders and descend-
ers to sweep way beyond their
neighbors, and joining strokes to
overlap. Long accustomed to such
paradoxes, Matthew designed the
Compressed Series and Snell at the
same time. "I used to work on one
in the morning, the other in the afternoon."

►A page
from Charles
Snell's
engraved
handwriting
manual,
London,
1714.

He looks at each new technology in terms of the problem/op-
portunity presented. By understanding the principles of the equipment, designers often uncover advantages that the engineers might
not have realized. With his next slides, he explained the hidden
virtues of the VIP machines:

"The writing lens of the VIP was driven by a stepping motor,
unlike the older Linofilm's constant motion. This was profound
to the typographer: By leaving the lens still, an accent could be
superimposed with absolute precision over a character." He showed
us slides of a particularly well suited non-Latin typeface that he'd
designed.

"Here's a syllable of a few different characters of Devanagari, an
Indian script. If you explode that
syllable into its component parts,
you can see how it's actually made
up as it's photocomposed."

Matthew continued, describing
yet another turnover in typesetting. "The Linotron 505 was Mergenthaler's first commercial typesetter, a half-photo, half-digital
hybrid. Each font was stored as
characters on a glass plate; the plate
was scanned and exposed in raster lines on a CRT (cathode ray
tube). It took a long time to change

►Devanagari,
an Indian
script
designed for
the VIP.

Design and Technology

▶Video K
before and
after
electronic
obliquing.

plates, that is, to change from one font to another. So instead of changing plates for italic, condensed, or expanded fonts, the owners of the typesetters saved time by using the CRT beam to oblique, shrink, or stretch the roman."

Because this had a particularly bad effect on Helvetica, Matthew created Video, a sans serif with stroke weights and curve shapes that compensated for the effects of electronic distortion. He designed not only for a particular technology, but for the ways in which people used it.

Matthew ventured into the present with the next slide. "It's important to make sure that a font for a video screen is compatible in set width with the same font for a printer or typesetter, so that when you display text on the screen, it will maintain consistent hyphenation and justification on the printer or typesetter. The lower-resolution 'bit-map' characters are derived from high-resolution outlines, so that what you see on the screen copyfits with

▶Character-
editing
program from
Interleaf, Inc.

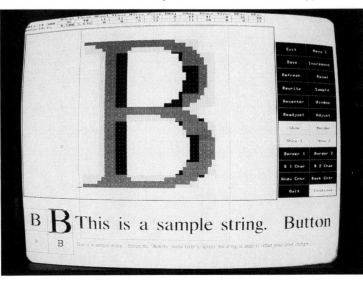

what you get on the printer and/or the typesetter. This slide shows a program that allows you to overlay the same character in different resolutions. You can see the resolution for the printer in the dark gray cap B; the lighter gray is the resolution for the video screen."

John pours me another cup of coffee, and I refocus my attention on the PC screen. One of the strongest features of their software—the ability to stretch and shrink text right along with the graphics—is also the most damaging to the characters. The more things change, the more they stay the same; it's so much like the tricks of the Linotron 505. Steven prints out a page from the screen, using a dot matrix printer that duplicates the screen's font. Unfortunately, they have a lot of work in store to make their type compatible with any other printer or typesetter. As I think about the complexity of my friends' task, I remember Matthew's closing remark:

"Technology is perfectible, humans are not, and most readers are still human."

14

·········

Electronic Rental Studios

Cynthia's company uses slide services now and then for presentations. When she saw an advertisement for a seminar using computer graphics equipment, she signed up, figuring it would help her to understand what options the service could provide.

The course turned out to be more useful than she expected.

Long after, the marketing director of her company came into the design department with a request for a slide show. For tomorrow. Cynthia called the place that they normally use, and got a quote for a rush job. It was exorbitant, and when she told the marketing director, he blanched. As they spread the slides from the last presentation over the light table, desperately trying to piece together something sensible, she remembered the course she had taken a few months earlier.

Graduates of the course were qualified to rent time on the equipment. Should she risk making the slides by herself? Why not? If she botched the job, the worst that could happen would be a short show of last year's slides. If she was successful, they'd have a new presentation and she could push for her raise.

Electronic Rental Studios

The marketing director was more than willing to risk $400 to rent the studio for four hours. (His boss had seen last year's slides too many times.) He gave her the copy he'd written for the word slides and the numbers for the charts.

Cynthia called the place where she had taken the course and asked if she could rent time that afternoon. She was afraid that the place would be booked, but they treated her as her doctor does when she frantically calls about strep throat. "OK, we can take care of you if you come over right now."

On her way out of the office, she grabbed a copy of her company's new annual report.

At the studio, the person who had taught her tutorial gave her a few refresher tips, then left her alone to work.

Cynthia had made word slides and charts during the course, so she already had a procedure. She started by setting up a master slide on the video screen. She created a grid, selected a typeface and several point sizes, and made a color palette for the type, the backgrounds, and the charts. From time to time, she asked her teacher to come in and make sure she was proceeding correctly. She wasn't used to doing so much work and "transmitting" it to a slide film recorder without actually touching any real materials. When she finished all the chart and word slides, there was about a half hour of studio time left. She flipped through the annual report, tearing out pages of the company's products, people, anything that would make a nice background for type. She put them under the video camera, scanned them onto the screen, and overlaid type to make title slides. She left the studio with two rolls of slide film.

She dropped the film off at the photo lab, bypassed her aerobics class, and went directly for the Jacuzzi.

There's a range of electronic studios where you can rent time to use equipment that you can't afford to buy, don't need to buy, or don't yet know enough about to buy.

On the lower end, the studios are equipped with personal computers, laser printers, and copiers. Even if your only purpose is to get a firsthand education, the costs are hard to resist.

Your first hour, which consists of training, is free. From then on it's about 15 dollars an hour, and about a dollar a page from the laser printer—cheaper with lower-quality paper or up to 2 dollars for 24-pound vellum.

The training session gives you a general overview of how to use basic features, like word processing, selection of typefaces, placement of type on a page, and creation of rules, shapes, and tints. This gives you a general feel for using the equipment, and from then on, you learn quickly by trial and error. When I tried it, the first thing I wanted to see was big type. After about 15 minutes I managed to get 5-inch-high letters on the laser printer.

♦ Update: Now that more software is available on personal computers, there is an abundance of places where you can rent time. Many service bureaus rent time and teach courses. See appendix A.

It definitely beat press type for cost and time, but it didn't match a typositor. This studio has a typesetter on order that will provide typeset quality of whatever you produce on the laser printer. (The studio has been expecting it since last summer.)

The higher-end studios have, in general, full-color workstations with a varying selection of typefaces and point sizes (depending on the choice of the equipment manufacturers), video cameras, color plotters, and film recorders. This is the kind that Cynthia used for her slides. Her tutorial cost $500, and the hourly rental fee is approximately $100 to $200 per hour, depending on the equipment and the amount of support you need. Not too many electronic rental studios exist yet, but the idea is quickly catching on.

By the way, Cynthia picked up her slides the next morning. The new presentation is great, much better than last year's. So's her paycheck.

15

Design Management

The Design Management and the Computer conference, held in Cambridge, Mass., in February, 1986, comprised three days and evenings of lectures, demonstrations, and visits to computer graphics companies.

Each afternoon, the attendees were given choices of what to attend. For instance, we could hear either John Waters's lecture, "Expanding the Possibilities of Design with the Computer," or Marc Fleischmann's talk, "System Needs Assessment, Selection, and Justification." Or we could go clothes shopping in Harvard Square.

I already have experience buying clothes in Harvard Square, but I certainly could use some pointers on what it takes to buy a computer graphics system, so I went to Marc's talk. There were only four or five people. Where was everybody? They were all listening to John Waters. If they were so interested in buying equipment, why was Marc's attendance so small, and John's so large?

A couple of weeks after the conference I went to visit Earl Powell, the director of the Design Management Institute, located in Boston. He explained the goals of the institute. I focused on four words that he used: awareness, comprehension, conviction, and action.

We talked about the imbalance of attendance between John's and Marc's talks, and I thought about those four words. Naturally, all of the attendees were aware of computer-based tools for design. That's why they came to the conference in the first place. Many comprehended what the tools could do. But few were convinced that computers were really useful. They wanted to see proof from someone who has already taken action.

DESIGN MANAGEMENT

The Design Management Institute is as much about managing as it is about designing, and so was the conference. Twenty-three speakers described products that fell into those two categories: computer-based tools for design management and for design development—as Earl describes it, a combination of the B school and the D school.

Tools is a key word. Like any tool, a computer just sits there until you do something with it. It's like a telephone. You can't just look at it and get your mother on the phone; you have to dial her number. There are telephones that you can program so that you only have to push one button and the number will automatically be dialed. You take the time to set up the system because you are convinced that it will save time in the long run.

The most obvious example of a computer-based tool for design management is DesignSoft, a software system for the tracking, billing, and management of project fees and expenses. Highgate Cross & Cathey is a design firm that developed this system for its own needs, and now the company is marketing it. Brad Cathey pointed out early in his talk that "the most important thing is to have a good manual system first. And we still do a lot of planning on paper."

So why use a computer when you have to set it all up on paper anyway?

One of the best things a computer does is compute. How many times have you added columns of numbers with your calculator, only to repeat the process the next day because one of the numbers was wrong, or something had to be changed? You don't want to sit down with your calculator each time numbers change in a project. And you may not want to wait until the end of a project to check on your current cash flow. You want to keep an up-to-the-minute total of all these elements of a job. Every time you change a number in DesignSoft, it automatically recalculates.

Brad has another argument for putting a job-tracking system on a computer. He says that it has encouraged people to *use* a system. The computer acts as a prompter. As long as you fill in the blanks, you get the numbers you want. (Well, maybe not the numbers you want, but the ones you need.)

If you are willing to invest the initial time to automate a good manual system, a computer-based tool helps in matters of financial information.

But what about using computers for design development, the D school side of graphic design?

DESIGN DEVELOPMENT

The title of Bill Haueisen's talk was "New Research Technology Saves Design Guesswork." Bill is the president of NOVA Research, a market research company that uses computers in many areas of its work.

One of the tools it uses is an *eye movement recorder.* This device tracks pupil movement. Let's say you're going to the supermarket for a jar of peanut butter. There are five different brands; which one will you buy? If you are the subject of a market research test of peanut butter labels, you look at a display of a variety of peanut butter jars, and the device records where your pupil looks and how long it stops at each jar.

"We can play back the tape and quantify how long each design element is looked at. This is enormously useful in evaluating different designs ... and gives us statistical reliability," Bill said.

I felt the audience squirm. Someone said, "I wish you had some doubts about your methods. ... These techniques, used without enough sensitivity to context, are harmful to intelligent approaches to design."

Just because the red jar gets the longest looks doesn't mean that you should design the next peanut butter label in red.

Clearly, a designer must decide when a procedure is a harness rather than an aid. Take a grid. The way you use it determines whether you help or ruin a design. (When I first heard the term *gridlock,* I didn't know it was a kind of traffic jam in New York City. I thought it was a reference to graphic designers who couldn't stop pretending they had gone to Yale.)

After a morning of lectures I was really ready for lunch. I sat down with a designer and soon found that the highlights of these conferences are the conversations with other people. I told her I'd been thinking about the structure that these computers impose on your work. I asked her if she felt that working with a computer could give you more freedom than working without one.

"Definitely! Just before I came here, I realized I had almost run out of business cards. I've been meaning to design a new card for two years. I really wanted to do something different. I wanted to take the time to try different typefaces, maybe some patterns, different colors, maybe even a photograph, and do a new letterhead, too. But I really didn't have time to go through the routine of collecting all the pieces and going through all the processes with all my suppliers. I ended up reprinting a short run of my old cards.

"In other words, the structure that I have right now inhibits my work.

"Last night I went to one of the demonstrations, and I saw just what I wanted. I would have been able to experiment with typefaces, colors, and photographs at one sitting. Unfortunately, I could never afford a system like that. So this afternoon I'm going to see what I can do with the cheaper systems."

Later that day, I wandered into the demonstration room. There was my lunch partner, sitting at one of the terminals. She was typing letters on the keyboard and moving the mouse around on the desk. I looked over her shoulder at the screen; there were four different business cards, each with a slight variation of type, point size, and placement. A few had patterns and rules of different weights.

During this conference, her position had changed from awareness to comprehension. I didn't want to interrupt her to ask if she was convinced.

IS ANYBODY READY TO TAKE ACTION?

One evening I spoke with Paul Brainerd, the founder and president of Aldus, the company that produces PageMaker, a page layout program that designers are starting to use on Macintosh computers. Paul mentioned that years ago he'd been president of a user's group for a computer-aided publishing system. A user's group is exactly what its name implies; it consists of companies that have bought a particular system and have established a group that meets to discuss the problems and/or missing features of the system. The system manufacturer listens very carefully to this group, because its members are the ones who actually use the product, and they often know much more about what it can and should do than the manufacturers themselves.

I got a phone call recently from an art director in Texas who is way beyond the early stages of awareness, comprehension, and conviction. He has definitely taken action. He has a lot to say about the work that his group is doing using computer-based tools, and he wants to share his experiences with other designers who are equally active. He needs a user's group. But he's having trouble finding anyone who would qualify as a member.

The best way for a designer to influence the development of computer-based design tools, and to take full advantage of those tools, is to become involved in that four-step process of awareness, comprehension, conviction, and action.

◆ Update: Many designers now have accounting and project-tracking software to make important facts about their business more accessible. See chapter 30, "The Business Side."

16

Disk Crashes

In November I started to worry about my taxes, so I got an accountant. She told me to make any equipment purchases before the end of the year because of the ITC. I thought, why would an accountant know about type, and what has that got to do with taxes? She went on to explain that it was a good time to take advantage of the investment tax credit. So I bought a computer and a printer in December.

I also bought a hard disk.

To keep whatever you've created on the computer screen, you have to store it, usually on a magnetic disk. There are different kinds of disks; the most important aspect is the amount of information that the disk can hold. Hard disks have much more storage space than floppy disks. I bought a hard disk because it's more convenient and faster to use than floppy disks. So instead of having to go through a shoe box full of disks every time I work on a different job, I can get it directly from one disk.

Storing your work is just like putting it away in a file cabinet, and it takes no more than a few keystrokes or mouse clicks. The difference is, when you put your work in a file cabinet, you know it's there. You can see it and touch it. When you store your work on a 5¼-inch piece of plastic, it doesn't feel quite safe. Nor should it. It's not uncommon for something to go wrong with a disk, and you can easily lose hours of work. (I print everything on paper, even before I've finished whatever I'm working on. It makes me feel better. Soon after I bought my computer I had to buy three file cabinets.)

One of the first rules of using a computer is to make *backups* of your disks. You simply copy the work that's on your original disk onto another. Then if something goes wrong with one disk, you have a perfect copy, an exact replica. When you have a hard disk, you back up onto individual floppies. Because you can store so much on a hard disk, it's even more important to back up your work. If you don't, and the disk "crashes," you could lose days of work.

I should have known when I bought this disk that it had a particularly high risk of failure: It had just been introduced to the market. Computer companies are extremely competitive. They are constantly trying to leapfrog each other with new products. As a result, they sometimes sell hardware or software that's full of mistakes and poorly documented. The customer is the guinea pig, and pays for it.

But this disk was cheaper than the other brand, so I bought it.

I used my computer, hard disk, and printer for months without any problems, other than investing hours figuring out how to print text so that it lined up correctly on my letterhead. Then one night, when I was finishing a report, it happened. The lights dimmed. I should have taken it as a warning, and backed up my work right then, but I didn't do that. Two minutes later, all the lights went off, and so did my computer. I looked out the window, and the buildings up and down the street were dark. There was nothing I could do; my typewriter is electric, too.

The next morning the power was back. My computer was OK, but I couldn't access anything on the hard disk. It was like losing the key to the file cabinet. No, it was like losing the file cabinet.

Thank God I had printed a rough draft of my report. Still, I felt sick at the thought of having to type it all over again. I looked in "Trouble Shooting," the thinnest section of the manual. Nothing. Then I called Robert Hafer, a local authority on such matters. I think of him as my doctor. If you have a computer, you need a doctor—preferably one who makes house calls.

Robert came right over. I sat behind him and watched as he, too, searched in vain for all the work on the hard disk. He recommended a hardware specialist. So I took the disk to a computer store's service department, and the people there said I probably had lost all the work that had been stored.

"But surely you backed up all your work?" they asked, knowing I hadn't. I hated them for rubbing it in like that.

They promised to have the hard disk fixed in two days. I re-typed my report, stored it on a floppy disk, and made two back-ups. I printed it four times even though I needed only one extra. Three days later I called the service department people. The manufacturer didn't have the part they needed. After two weeks, I began to suspect that I was low on their priority list. I called every other day, and they were always with "a customer." (I've learned that a customer is someone who is just about to buy a computer.)

After a month I finally got my hard disk back, as good as new. Actually, as bad as new. It was swept clean of everything I'd stored.

That was two months ago. Since then I've been pretty careful about making backups on floppies, so that if anything else happens to my disk, I'll have the work I need.

P.S. Yesterday some of my relatives were in town, and I brought them by to see my computer. It was the middle of the day and the lights weren't on, so this time I didn't have any warning before my hard disk crashed.

♦ Update: When designers first started using computers, a 20-megabyte hard disk was more than adequate. Now that we're storing more typefaces and pages, as well as data-intensive pictures, an 80-megabyte disk fills up before you know it!

Realistic Expectations

Chris describes her design for the sign system of a 200-acre industrial park as High Industrial: large scale, bright colors, repetition, and lots of metal and chain link. The park has a very eclectic range: There's a shipyard on one side, and a new design center across the street.

There were a lot of factors to consider in the design. What was the correct scale? What were the right colors? How many signs should there be? How close together? How will the whole thing look? Chris wanted to mix real images of the existing space with the proposed signs. She wanted to create a streetscape.

She had seen demonstrations of computer graphics systems, and felt that this was a perfect use, a clear match of her needs with the system's capabilities. She would use the slides she had taken of the site, create the graphics on the system, and superimpose the graphics over the image of the site, all right on the screen. She could experiment with different sizes, colors, and placement on the screen, then produce 35mm slides to use for her client presentation. The presentation would show an extremely realistic view of the site with the proposed signs in place.

At least that's what she thought.

She brought in the pictures of the site and her "paper sketches," color key mock-ups of the various panels. She didn't have time to learn how to use the system, so she "art-directed" the operator. They digitized the picture using the system's video camera, and the image appeared on the screen. Chris thought, "It certainly doesn't look crisp. Oh well, it's on a video screen. It will look better on the final slide."

It was easy to create the graphics for the panels directly on the system's screen. The operator created colored rectangles, triangles, and circles in a few seconds, and added type at an angle simply by typing on the keyboard, selecting a typeface, and indicating the angle of rotation. Unfortunately, they didn't have a wide selection of typefaces, so they had to use Helvetica, even though the actual signs will be in Univers. They placed the graphics at various locations and sizes over the image of the site. The panels looked bright, crisp, and clear. The type and graphics on the sign that was a hundred yards away were as readable as the ones ten feet away.

That was the problem. Nobody's eyes are that good. The graphics were *too* clear. The type was too sharp, the colors too bright, the edges too precise. It made the picture of the site look even fuzzier, more washed out, less crisp. The contrast made the lower quality of the image even more obvious.

They removed the type from the distant panels; that didn't help much. The operator suggested scanning the paper sketches, hoping that they would be more in keeping with the photographs of the site. But the graphics still looked awkward, and very unrealistic. The panels looked exactly like what they were: flat artwork. The perspective wasn't quite right, they had no dimension, and the color was too consistent: no shadows or variations in tone.

Chris wanted to see how the images they had created on the screen would look on slides. They transmitted the images from the screen to the film recorder, then sent the film out for processing. When they looked at the slides, the difference between the real photographs of the site and the graphics that were made on the computer was even more severe. They discussed the problem, and Chris learned some important details.

When a picture is digitized using a video camera, the image is typically recorded at the same resolution as the video screen. That's all you're recording, and you can't get more detail back. There are big, expensive scanners that record images at very high resolution, much higher than the video screen. But these machines are used

▶Chris scanned a 35mm slide of an existing site, then created the signage elements on the computer. The resulting images look unrealistic.

for production work, and they are cost-effective for color separators and printers, not designers.

Chris's graphics were flat colors, so it was natural that they would look sharper than the photographic images. This mix of vocabularies would be evident in any medium, not just computer graphics. However, the type on the slides was even sharper than the graphics.

Type is stored in the computer as an outline. The outline is not actually drawn and filled in until it is displayed on the screen or exposed on film. When it's displayed on the screen, it's the same resolution as everything else. But when the image of the screen is transferred to slide film, the type is redrawn at a much higher resolution. The final slides have low-resolution images and high-resolution type.

Chris found that the computer was a great tool for experimenting with scale and placement, and it gave her a better feel for the overall look of the design. But she decided not to use the slides from the system for her presentation to the client. The presentation had to have one "reality," not a mixture. She used her traditional techniques.

▶Chris decided that it was better to have one "reality," so she used traditional materials (copier, markers, colored paper, and so on) for her presentation.

Realistic Expectations

It's hard to tell whether a computer graphics system will meet your needs just from watching a demonstration. A canned demo shows the system off to its best advantage with carefully edited source materials. Ask the vendor some questions and provide some information before you begin the job:

What is the best form for the original artwork? (Chris's pictures of the site were slides. She would have had sharper, more detailed images if they had digitized Cibachromes or, better yet, 8 x 10 transparencies.)

What are the available typefaces?

What is the range of colors?

What kind of hard copy is available?

What is the resolution of the final hard copy? (Ask for a description in terms that you're familiar with, such as video resolution versus print resolution.)

Describe what you intend to use the work for, and how large you intend to reproduce the work.

Ask for samples that are similar to your job.

Show them your original artwork that you plan to digitize.

Allot some time for understanding the capabilities of the system as it pertains to your particular plans.

And no matter what they show you in a demo, don't expect magic.

Type for Environmental Design

When you see a company's sign, you are looking at part of its visual identity program. Many signs are translations of printed pieces, bigger-than-life versions of the letterhead. The sign might be an interior graphics system, a trade show display, or a building sign, fabricated out of sheet metal, structural steel, plastic, molding, woodwork; it may be spray-painted or applied. But creating a sign system consistent with the print material is not as easy as specing type. Signs are not made at a type shop on a typesetter; a sign has to be created as a unique piece, drawn and fabricated individually.

Until a few years ago, typesetting and sign manufacturing were two completely different worlds. The letterforms for typesetters were stored in the typesetting machine as photographic masters or, in digital typesetting, as many tiny dots that make up the shapes of characters. These characters were exposed to photographic paper

Type for Environmental Design

or film. In sign manufacturing, typefaces were not "stored"; they were traced or drawn from artwork, and cut by hand. There were relatively few typefaces used in sign manufacturing, especially compared to the thousands used in print.

▶With digital masters of outline type, the computer can draw and cut characters at any size.

Typesetting technology continues to advance at an accelerated rate, and one of its recent developments is having a big effect on the sign manufacturing industry: digital outline type masters (see chapter 2, "Digital Type Masters"). Each character master in a font can be stored as an outline in the computer, the "front end" of the typesetting system. In addition to the actual shape of each character, the computer can store all the typesetting instructions for size and placement of each character, and send those instructions to the "back end," the output machine, where the type is finally set. There is a wide range of output machines—not just typesetters—that use type in this form, including video systems, computer-aided design systems, and slide-making systems, to name a few.

When the sign manufacturing industry was introduced to this technique for describing characters, its practitioners immediately saw the implications for their own work. Type that was previously produced (drawn, traced, and cut) by hand can now be generated and cut by a computer.

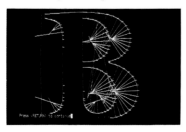
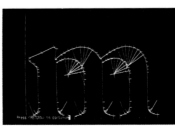

▶The characters are stored in the computer as mathematical descriptions of lines and curves.

An example of a digital type foundry that was formed specifically to produce digital type, Bitstream Inc. creates digital type masters for these new computer-controlled output technologies. Bitstream delivers the digital masters to its customers, who then install the masters on their systems. One of Bitstream's customers is Cybermation, a company that has developed a turnkey computer system for sign manufacturing.

When Bitstream delivers fonts to a customer, it requests that the client provide sample characters from his or her machine. This is an important step in letterform quality control. Typically, Bitstream's customers send character samples on paper or film, from such machines as printers or typesetters. But Cybermation created a novel set of sample characters: the letters spelling Bitstream, cut out of $1\frac{1}{2}$-inch-thick Plexiglas with a 26-inch cap height.

Cybermation sells its system, complete with the type library, to the sign manufacturing companies. One of Cybermation's customers, University Brink, is owned and operated by the Sawyer family and has been manufacturing signs since 1866. The firm purchased its Cybermation system about seven months ago and is using the system for about 50 percent of its work; traditional techniques account for the other 50 percent.

Cybermation's sign-making process presents a unique opportunity to explain how the computer has modernized this part of the environmental design industry.

SIGN FABRICATION

The sign fabrication activity at University Brink takes place in a vast area that houses huge three-dimensional letters, an occasional truck with a 100-foot aerial crane used for installing the signs, and miscellaneous pieces of equipment from various eras in sign manufacturing.

Traditional Method

Tom Delman, a member of University Brink's art department, explains the traditional way of making three-dimensional letters:

Type for Environmental Design

"First I get a sketch from the client. I enlarge it by eye, because I have an art background. Another technique is to project the sketch on the wall at the final size I want, and trace the projection. There are some problems with projection. It can introduce distortion. And if you have a really large letter, you will need a huge empty room.

"In the old days, we used to wait till it was dark to draw the letters. We would take the projector outside to somebody's house that had a long driveway, and project the letter on the side of the garage. Still, a lot of the work is done by projection."

Once the shape is defined, it is prepared for cutting. "When we have the shape right, we perforate it with a perforating wheel, a wheel pouncer." (Think of the miniature version of the tool used to make clothing patterns.) Once the entire letter has its perforated pattern, it is sent to the "metal men," the union that does the cutting of the letters out of metal.

To transfer the pattern onto the metal, the metal men "dust" a pounce bag of charcoal (similar to using a powder puff) over the perforations, so that the charcoal comes through to show the pattern. "Actually, they have replaced the charcoal, which is very bad for the lungs, with baby powder," continues Delman. Then they remove the perforated sheet, revealing the metal with the pattern. Next, a bit of hairspray is used to keep the baby powder from blowing away–some pretty delicate tools for such a hefty business.

With the pattern completed, they can cut out the letter using either a saber saw or a band saw, depending on whether the letters are primarily straight or round.

Delman pointed to a pile of about 15 letters, each about two feet tall, and said, "It took about 20 minutes to cut each letter, and a really good cutter did that. The new computer system could cut the whole set of letters in 20 minutes.

"Think of the guy who has to cut 15 signs, and they are all supposed to be exactly the same. By the 10th letter, he is getting pretty tired, and makes a mistake. With the computer, the 15th one will be exactly the same as the first. It is exact duplication."

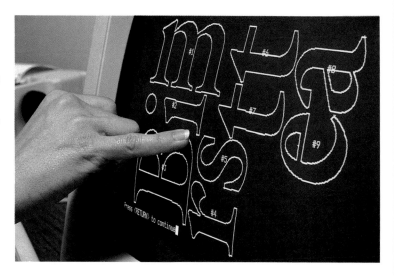

▶Because the letters will be cut as individual items, they are "nested." This process rearranges the letters to minimize waste of material.

Computer Method

University Brink's new equipment includes an operator's workstation, a video screen, a keyboard, a mouse, a small pen plotter that provides a paper proof of whatever is on the screen, a big pen plotter that provides an actual-size paper copy of the job, and, finally, the actual computer—the part of the system that stores all the information and software programs—which sits humming under the desk. All these pieces of equipment are connected to each other by cables. The computer is also cable-connected to the machine in another room that cuts out the letters.

A typical work session begins with the screen asking the operator a few questions. What is the gauge size? (This refers to the length and width of the material from which the letters will be cut.) Will the letters remain or will it be a stencil cut? This determines whether there will be lead-in or lead-out. (Think about cutting a shape out of a piece of paper: If you are using the inside of a letter, you cut in from the outside; if you are using the background, you cut from the inside.) What are the dimensions of the letters? The sign industry does not communicate in point sizes; its sizes are based on the height of a cap *A*.

Type for Environmental Design

The operator types at the keyboard, and the letters appear on the screen in outlines. The computer screen prompts: "Nesting?"

The *nesting* program rearranges the letters, turning them sideways and upside down, fitting them as closely together as possible so that the least amount of material is used—much like planning page composition in offset printing. The materials for signs are often the most expensive component of a job. It is important to use the material in the most efficient manner when letters are cut as individual shapes.

If the letters are to be cut or drawn as one word, letterspacing is important. Using a mouse, the operator selects a letter and moves the mouse over the desk, while the letter moves correspondingly on the screen.

Because the letter is stored as an outline, there are manipulations you can achieve: You can scale the characters horizontally or vertically, and you can slant them or make mirror images of them. Everything you specify you can see on the screen, although the computer takes a few seconds to "think" it out first.

Once the instructions for typeface, size, and arrangement are stored in the computer, the operator can send the information to any number of output devices, or choose any number of attachments, or cut out of any number of materials.

Individual material costs and weights are entered into the system, and the computer calculates the cost and weight of the letters, based on the material he or she specifies. Finally, the computer tells the operator how long it will take to cut a letter or a series of letters.

The machine that actually cuts the letters has a bed (actually, a vacuum table) that is 8 feet wide by 12 feet long. Rail extensions extend the length up to 24 feet. This means you could cut one letter 8 x 24 feet, if you could find a sheet of material that big or a letter that skinny.

The attachments available for use with the cutting machine depend on the material that is being cut. One is a plasma cutting tool, a heated gas that will cut just about any metal carbon and stainless

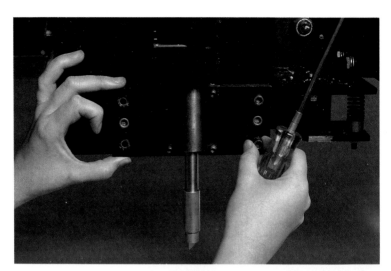

► To cut letters out of a thin adhesive material like vinyl, a blade attachment is used.

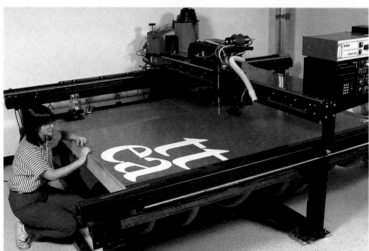

► Ann Wojcicki, from the applications department, places the vinyl on the plotter and turns on the vacuum.

steels, aluminum, brass, and bronze.

If the material being cut is a vinyl or plastic film with adhesive backing, the appropriate attachment is an air spring-loaded knife. The knife floats on a regulated air cushion to maintain an even cutting pressure. The air pressure is controlled depending on the thickness of the material. (Think about when you are cutting a Rubylith®, and how you try to achieve just the right pressure.)

Type for Environmental Design

▶As the letters are cut out of the Plexiglas, the drill bit gets very hot. Ann sprays the bit with an oil-based solution.

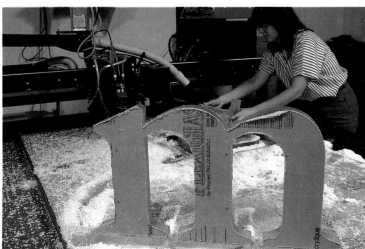

▶When the Plexiglas letters are cut out, the protective paper can be peeled off.

Varying sizes of router bits can be attached for cutting wood or plastic or metals. Pens are used to draw plots on paper for scale drawings.

After the operator chooses and inserts the correct attachment for the cutting machine, and places the material in position, he or she types a few commands at the keyboard and the machine begins to cut the letters. If the material is thick Plexiglas, the operator monitors the cutting. But if the material is thin and simple, he or she is free to start working on the next job or, better yet, take a coffee break.

19

Varied Tasks

You've decided to buy a computer system, but you haven't started to look yet.

Do you intend to use it for varied tasks, such as accounting, word processing, job costing, time management, and simple, nearly typeset-quality type and graphics? Or will you buy a *dedicated system* for a specific graphic arts application, such as a system to produce high-volume technical documentation, or a multimedia system to produce full-color slides or video?

This chapter is about issues that you should consider if you're buying a system that accommodates a variety of tasks. The factors are different for a dedicated system (see the next chapter).

The hardware that you'll probably be buying—personal computer(s), printer(s), hard disk(s)—may be from one company, or it may be from several. Different software packages come from different companies: accounting software from one company, graphics programs from another, and so on. You'll be collecting information and/or advice about hardware and software products from salespeople, consultants, suppliers, and colleagues. It's up to you to determine which considerations are more important than others.

Cost of the Components

Is cost the most important factor? Many design studios have a limited budget, and a good copier is more crucial than a computer.

If your priority is to keep your costs low, you'll probably buy one computer and a simple, letter-quality printer. Can you afford more sophisticated peripherals? An elaborate setup can link several computers, plus a laser printer, more storage capacity, a modem for transferring information over the telephone, and so on. If you have a large budget, the cost should be a less important consideration than other items on your list.

Cost to Upgrade Hardware and Software

Most companies come out with new products or new versions of their products every year. How much will it cost to upgrade to the new system? Some companies provide upgrades at a minimal cost, some charge a lot, and some charge for versions that are simply corrections to the bugs in the older software.

Variety of Software Available

Some personal computers are very advanced, with excellent graphic capabilities and a low price. But not much software is available for them, unless they are compatible with more popular computers. One of the reasons that IBM and Apple sell so much is *because* they sell so much. And the more they sell, the more software products are developed for them. So if you plan to use the system for a lot of different tasks, you need to consider the software that's available.

Reliability and Repair Service

A computer may have a good price and a lot of features, but also a bad reputation for hardware failures. The same is true for software programs. If your work requires fast turnaround and high volume, you can't afford to have a temperamental system that loses your work. But even with the most reliable product, something is bound to go wrong. Where is the closest service department? Is the system so obscure that it has to be shipped out of state? How long will it take to get it repaired? Are items in stock? Can you rent a temporary replacement?

Service Contracts

Computers have various lengths of time for warranties. After the warranty has expired, you can usually buy a service contract. This is basically health insurance for your computer. You pay a flat yearly rate, and you're covered. Some service contracts apply only to the store where you bought the equipment. If you buy the manufacturer's service contract, you can get repairs at any store, but you'll be lower on the repair list than the customer with the store's service contract.

Customer Support

Sometimes it's hard to tell if something is broken or if you've simply pressed the wrong button. How good is the company's customer-support department? Does it have a customer hotline? Is it a toll-free number? Is it always busy? This has become a difficult problem for software manufacturers, because they continue to have costs way after they've sold the product. User's groups, people who have bought the same kind of computer or who have the same interests, can be more helpful and even more knowledgeable about a product. New York, for example, has a Macintosh user's group—known by the unappetizing acronym NYMUG. The Boston Computer Society has a large number of special interest groups, from lawyers to nonprofit organizations to publishers.

Backup Supplier and Equipment

Is there a convenient supplier who has a service with the same equipment as yours? If your laser printer breaks down, where can you get printouts while waiting for your machine to be repaired?

Leading-Edge vs. Mature, Proven Technology

Do you want to be the first kid on the block to have the latest technology, or would you prefer to wait and learn from someone else's mistakes? You may even consider buying used equipment, as long as it's not obsolete and without a place for supplies, peripherals or repairs.

Learning Time

Do you plan to have one person who will use the system all the time and be the office guru? Or do you plan to have a number of more casual users? Some systems are easier to learn, and are accessible more quickly.

Friends

Finally, find out what your friends and colleagues have bought. Chances are you'll learn more from each other than you will from a salesperson, and your shared discoveries will be ongoing.

20

A Dedicated System

I get a lot of calls from people who say, "I've been assigned the project of choosing a computer system for our department. What should I get?"

First, get a raise. Better yet, get some help. It's a hard job, and if you're expected to accomplish it along with the four color brochures coming up, you'll need some assistance. Second, read this. It will give you a place to start.

In the last chapter, I made a list of things you should consider if you want to buy a computer that can be used for a lot of different tasks, such as word processing, accounting, and producing nearly typeset-quality text and graphics. The basic components of this kind of system are a personal computer, a printer, and various software packages.

This chapter deals with the dedicated system, which is devoted to streamlining the process for *one* graphic arts application. For instance, a system for comprehensive technical manuals will have features to repeat the layout, running heads, folios, and so forth automatically for thousands of pages. But it's cumbersome when you try to do something unique on a page, such as wrapping text around an illustration. A system for making newspaper ads favors unique elements, and minimizes the multipage features.

When you start looking, don't waste your time with systems not ideally suited to your work. Be pushy about getting very realistic demonstrations.

COST OF THE SYSTEM

One of the first things you'll have to do is present a budget. You know that awful feeling you get when you quote a design job, and during the job a number of unexpected expenses come up? Assume the worst when you assemble all the costs associated with a computer system, because there are so many alien factors. Ask salespeople for an exhaustive list of items and prices. Then ask again, because they will have overlooked many of the "little" items crucial to the system. Here are some of the things with separate price tags:

The basic workstation (monitor, keyboard, computer, tablet, stylus)

Additional workstations (A dedicated system is typically several workstations linked together.)

Network (a cable system linking the workstations)

Software (probably several programs)

Copies of software (Many vendors don't allow you to copy software; you have to purchase a new package for each workstation.)

Controller ("traffic cop" equipment that routes files from one machine to another)

Streamer tape (for backing up and archiving files)

Service contract (your system's health insurance)

Training (it's worth buying additional time)

Upgrades (new versions of the software and/or hardware)

Trade-up charges (You may be penalized for breaking a lease.)

More memory (Do you ever have enough file cabinets?)

Modems (to transmit files by telephone)

Supplies (disks, magnetic tape, photo paper, film)

Font library (a vital and expensive ingredient)

Scanner/video camera (input)

Printer, film recorder, color plotter, typesetter (output)

Film processor and chemicals (for a typesetter)

Environmental requirements (electrical power, physical space, air-conditioning)

Salary for a "system manager" (Keep reading.)

PERSONNEL

No matter how easy the system is to use, it will require a formidable change in the department's working methods. And even if your staff is eager, you should have a *system manager,* a person who is responsible for the equipment. This is no slouch job; it's a big responsibility. He or she should know how to use the system and be available to teach and help others, perform basic maintenance, and be the contact for the vendor. As a matter of fact, you should hire or designate that person before you purchase the system. A computer background isn't necessary. You'd be better off with someone who is sympathetic to the nontechnical design and production people. The best system manager I know majored in philosophy.

RELIABILITY

When I get bored with the technical articles in trade publications, I often turn to the financial section. It's amazing how many companies can get venture capital and within a few months file for bankruptcy. When examining equipment, look at the company selling it. How old is it? How big? How many installations does it have?

♦ Update:
Personal
computers,
peripherals,
and software
programs are
now much
more
powerful.
These con-
figurations
can perform
many of the
jobs that
were once
limited to
dedicated
systems.

If it goes out of business, you're out of luck.

Another potential problem: When a vendor promises you new versions of software, you may think, "Great. New features for free." You wish it. Being a test site is expensive when the software is full of bugs. Speaking of new software, I heard about an illustrator who created artwork on a computer graphics workstation, but when she tried to produce more samples a few months later, her old disks were incompatible with the new version of the system. It was like trying to put a record album on a CD player.

The task of choosing a computer graphics system can be intimidating. But you will quickly see it in the context of your work, and discover new opportunities for your business and creativity. If you fail to find a useful system, save your money. Don't climb a mountain just because it's there. The search is well worth the education, and when the new technology does have something to offer you, you'll be ready for it.

21
Real Type

The other day my car got towed, so I took a bus to the office. You can learn a lot when you have to stand in one place for 15 minutes with nothing to read but the stuff taped to the lamppost. One flier caught my eye.

"Desktop publishers: laser typesetting for your Macintosh from our Allied L100 typesetter. $15 per page. While you wait. Located next to McDonald's."

That seemed appropriate. Cheap type fast. I tore off one of the little tabs with the telephone number and stuck it in my appointment book.

I was already familiar with the basics of creating pages on the Macintosh and getting repro. I knew how many typefaces were available, and I knew the typesetter was a Mergenthaler. (The *L* stands for linotype.) I knew some of the benefits: You can compose and lay out all the typographic elements of a page–type, rules, and patterns–without using codes. The repro comes out of the typesetter with all the elements in place, so you cut down on pasteup. And I knew some of the drawbacks: The current selection of typefaces available for the Macintosh is limited; as of November 1986 there were only about 21 families. Most of the people using desktop publishing don't ask for much more than Times Roman and Helvetica. Bembo is just a silly word.

I had been using a Macintosh to play with different headlines and new wave patterns. I decided to do an experiment. When I got to the office, I called the laser type shop.

"How many fonts do you have?" I asked.

"About 40." (That means about 10 families.)

The person on the phone gave me a quick rundown of typeface names. His list included a few that were produced by typographically naive entrepreneurs. I told him that those didn't count as typefaces.

"That's true," he said, "not all of the fonts are old, historical typefaces like ITC."

Clearly his background was not typesetting.

He asked me some questions to make sure that my file would typeset correctly. "What program did you use? Do you have more than three fonts in your file? Did you set the Chooser to the LaserWriter instead of the ImageWriter? Did you proof the page on a LaserWriter?"

I felt like I was taking a test. My grade was barely above average: I did select the LaserWriter, and I did proof the page on the Laser-Writer. That was good. I used MacDraw, and a lot more than three fonts. That was bad.

"MacDraw's font menu is listed differently from other software," he explained. "This confuses the L100, and a complicated job won't set, so you have to load the MacDraw file into another program to stabilize it. And you can't use more than three fonts because there's a timing problem on the network; the fonts get in each other's way and there's a collision. But it can handle big type." He talked about the oversights of software developers and the temporary software fixes that you can buy for 50 dollars. He listed the programs that were due for revisions, and predicted which ones would be ready when.

He may not know type, but he sure knows his Mac.

I asked if he would make the necessary corrections on my disk. He said that would defeat the whole purpose of this kind of typesetting. "The type is cheap because it's hands-on for you, hands-off for us. We're not responsible for anything other than getting

Real Type

your file into the typesetter and pulling the repro out. You're responsible for the placement, the spelling, the spacing, the specing. … Basically, you're avoiding the cost of our labor."

I decided to simplify this experiment. I retyped the headlines in Microsoft Word, chose three styles of Palatino and made them 127 points high. I was tired of the patterns anyway. I stored the file on a spare floppy disk, put it in my pocket, and went to get my car from the tow lot.

Then I drove to the laser shop and got a space right in front of McDonald's. I went next door to a large, air-conditioned office, littered with Macintoshes. The typesetter was in the corner near the darkroom. I found the person I'd spoken to on the phone and handed over my disk. While the job was running, he talked about different software programs, Macintosh tricks, and new products from Apple. Within 15 minutes the job was set: a page of real type for 15 bucks, and I didn't even use up the parking meter.

I got back to the office and looked more closely at the repro. The characters were nice. It was, after all, Mergenthaler type. The spacing was so-so. This had nothing to do with the typesetter, and everything to do with the software program that I used to make the headlines; there was no way to modify the space between the letters. Desktop publishing programs are just starting to include built-in kerning and control of letterspacing and word spacing. And Palatino was OK, but I really wanted Bembo.

Laser typesetting for your Macintosh. It's real type, but not real typography.

Not yet, anyway.

♦ Update: The improvements in typographic control and typeface variety over the past three years have been overwhelming. This has its advantages and drawbacks. See chapter 37, "Computers in the Studio."

22

·········

Keeping Up with Your Clients

———

Anyone who's involved with computers gets a lot of mail. My mailbox is always stuffed, but I don't mind. I'm part of a direct mail information network, and there's usually something worth knowing about.

One day I received a direct mail piece from a company that makes page layout software for personal computers. The letter described its new product: a series of templates to be used with its program. The package, which costs $79, includes a workbook and 21 newsletter layouts on a disk. "All you have to do is place your text and graphics in pages already laid out by a group of professional designers." The letter goes on to say that the templates help nondesigners develop their design sense and skill to produce original work on their own.

I wanted to hear what other designers thought about this new product. I went to lunch with a friend who had cultivated an aversion to computers, and while we waited for our sandwiches I pulled out the envelope with the sample designs. At first he wouldn't even look. "I've heard about desktop publishing. It's just for publications that don't need quality typography." When I started to put away the envelope he said, "OK, OK, let's see."

His reaction went from smugness ("Look at that awful letterspacing and lousy rag right!") to bravado ("These designs are fine for people who can't afford to hire a designer. They're generic, safe, vanilla.") to fear ("But I do have a client who might use that.") to frustration ("Damn. Think about the huge return on investment this company will make from 21 simple design variations. It's a great idea. Why didn't I think of that?").

When his sandwich arrived he said he wasn't hungry.

A lot of designers boycott computers in an effort to protect fine typography. They say that tradition will disappear, erased from history like a Russian diplomat. In every new typesetting technology–from linotype to laser type–the finer points of character shape, kerning, letterspacing, and typeface selection are initially sacrificed in favor of getting the equipment to market. But the vast body of typographic knowledge that has been collected over generations is well documented. The problems of computer-aided typesetting are well documented. If you can articulate a problem, then it is practically solved. Producers of page layout programs are constantly adding new features. More kerning pairs. More typefaces. More alternate characters. More resolution. More sophisticated, built-in hyphenation dictionaries. More control. Typographic standards will be maintained by virtue of a competitive marketplace.

You provide much more than visual advice for your clients. You understand and you control their methods of production. Your clients don't know how to mark up type, specify stats, or make mechanicals.

Most of the designers who don't have a computer have clients who do. Graphic designers are not the target audience for companies that develop these sophisticated computer-aided publishing products; people who own computers are. You're the one who's supposed to be advising your clients about producing printed materials, but now software companies are telling them how to do production themselves.

Are your clients better informed about production than you are?

About six months after our lunch, my friend called to tell me what he'd been up to.

In lieu of money for a job, he asked his biggest client to supply him with a system identical to their own. Then he designed a corporate identity system—a canned format—that took advantage of the features of their software. Now his client's staff is starting to take over some of the production work that he used to do. But he hasn't had time to worry about that: Word travels, and he's getting work from other companies that are eager to maximize the use of their computers. He's approaching another client who uses a full-color workstation, so that he can design the color palette, typography, and layout for their slide presentations. As he learns about more computer graphic systems, he augments his repertoire of advice for other clients. His name must be on 50 mailing lists.

When I kidded him about his 180-degree turnaround, he responded in his typical manner. "I'm doing what I've always done. I'm providing my clients with the most efficient and creative design and production solutions."

The idea that computers will replace graphic designers is silly. Computers have generated more design jobs than they could possibly replace. Designers won't lose a job to a computer. They'll lose it the way they always have: to another designer who's a step ahead.

Have you checked your mailbox today?

♦ Update: Many designers are now taking advantage of their clients' use of computers by providing more sophisticated specifications. See chapter 31, "Design Tools."

23

Last Year's Budget

In 1984 a computer that could be used as a design tool was too expensive for most in-house design departments. Design managers had a hard enough time justifying a stat camera. How could they request a computer that cost ten times as much?

By 1987, computers became so inexpensive and popular that design managers barely had to ask and the purchase order was signed. Computers are popping up in design departments all over the country. Design managers can't ignore it. It's not enough to attract new design talent and clients by winning awards. Design students expect state-of-the-art design offices. Clients expect state-of-the-art turnaround.

But in their haste to get a computer into the department, design managers are neglecting the most important question:

What are the real costs of successfully using a computer in the design department?

I know a design director who purchased a computer for his department, and every time he looks at it he feels guilty. The computer has been sitting there for months, untouched. I asked him why he got it.

He said, "All the other departments were buying computers for word processing, accounting, direct mail. .... There's a computer on practically every desk. I didn't want the design department to be left out, so I stuck $3,000 in the budget. After we bought it, no one had time to figure out what to do with it. I finally spent some of my own time and I found out that we needed another $7,000 worth of stuff to make it useful."

Then he said something that sounded too familiar:

"They'd never let us spend that. It's way above our budget."

Where does that budget come from?

Design managers seem to have a fear of asking for more money than the design managers before them. Designers do themselves, their clients, and other designers a disservice when they continually underestimate their needs.

I remember the first time I had to submit an annual budget. After I totaled the figures, my first reaction was to reduce them. I spent hours going back over each item, figuring out how to do things cheaply. When I finally presented the budget to my boss, he said, "You're approaching this the wrong way. We have to figure out how much we need to be successful. If we underestimate, and don't start out with the appropriate funds, we're sure to fail."

That was an eye-opener. I rewrote the budget, including what I felt would allow us not only to do the work, but also to grow and take on more work, and be more profitable.

Before you decide to ask for a computer for your design department, you should have a clear idea of why you need it, and how the department will benefit.

Do you want to save money on typesetting? Do you want faster turnaround time on corrections? Do you want to be able to set type for comps in-house? Do you want to automate copyfitting? Do you want to make a mechanical without doing any pasteup? Do you have clients who need formats they can use with their computers?

Do you want to make color comps without using outside services? Do you want to create line art without rapidiographs, french curves, and stats?

Last Year's Budget

Do you want to automate your invoices? Are you looking for a better way to handle your accounting?

There are definitely areas in which a computer can help your department save a lot of time and money. But before you reap those benefits, you have to *spend* a lot of time and money.

When you submit your budget, you should know what you need to accomplish those tasks. Does the budget cover the ingredients? The computer itself—whether it's a lap-top or a mainframe—is cheap compared to the laundry list that goes with it.

What software packages should you buy? Word processing? Composition? Page layout? Paint? Line art? Photographic manipulation? Data base? Accounting? Communications? What typefaces?

What peripheral hardware will you need? Scanners? Video cameras? Color plotters? Modems? Laser printers? Film processors? Hard disks?

Do you need more space? More electricity? Extra phone lines? Service contracts?

And then there's the most important and costly ingredient of all: time.

The learning curve is very steep when you start to learn about and use a computer system. How much time does it take to do that research? Whose time? Where do you get the information? How many hours will each designer need to learn how to use it? A new heading is starting to appear in the budgets of design departments. It's called Research and Development. Who absorbs that cost? Do you charge the client? Is it overhead?

If you're a design manager who's decided that a computer will be a useful tool in the design department, make sure that you have budgeted the time and the ingredients. You won't grow if you limit yourself to last year's goals.

Don't look back.

♦ Update: Now that more designers are using computers, more numbers and information are available to justify your budget. See chapter 38, "The Bottom Line."

24

System Incompatibility

My living room has changed dramatically

in the past 24 hours. Yesterday I went with a friend to a huge warehouse sale of audio-video components. I had no intention of buying anything. I used to have a simple record player. Now I have a huge TV with giant rabbit ears, a VCR, a receiver, a turntable, a tape deck, a CD player, and four separate remote controls.

Four remote controls! I get the "Today" show when I want to listen to David Bowie. This morning I called the salesman who sold me the stuff.

"Why do I have four separate remote controls? They all look the same. Why can't I use just one?"

"Because." Heavy sigh. "They're not compatible."

A friend was designing an annual report for one of her regular clients. They used personal computers to write their copy and, with their encouragement, she used the computer to make comps.

She always hated specing tables, so she decided to try using the computer. Maybe she could even send the disk to the typesetter and avoid marking up the manuscript altogether. She tried a simple table, and proofed it on the laser printer. It looked OK, but she had to see it typeset; this was an annual report, and it had to be perfect. She sent the disk to her type shop. When she got the job back, it didn't look quite like the printout. Nor did it look like her type shop's usual level of quality. So she marked photocopies of the repro with corrections like "Add ½ point lead here" and "tighter overall letterspacing," and figured that she had saved a lot of time and money on the typesetting; these were minor corrections.

Her type shop called back and said, "You have to make those corrections yourself on the computer and send us a new disk file."

She was surprised, and said, "But you've always been able to make those corrections easily before."

"This job is set on a different system than the one we normally use for your jobs. They're not compatible."

In the past few chapters I've talked about the changes that personal computers are causing for designers. Clients use word processing software and regularly send designers manuscripts on disks instead of paper. Now clients are buying page layout software, and they are asking, with more and more frequency, that designers spec pages of type and graphics in a software program instead of on paper.

Designers are advisers. Now they have to advise their clients about using personal computers in production. They also have to explain to their clients when and why a personal computer is *not* appropriate.

The reality is that you can save a lot of time, money, and corrections and still get your type shop's expertise by sending text files. The dream is that you can get the same things when you send page files. There are substantial obstacles in between.

OBSTACLE ONE: PAGE DESCRIPTION LANGUAGES

Most type shops can accept an enormous range of word processing formats; they have equipment that will translate all the different formats into one that works with their typesetting equipment.

Page layout software is incredibly more complicated than straight text because it includes type specifications, placement, graphics,

Design and Technology

overlaps, reverses, rotations, patterns, and more. Each headline, rectangle, and tint screen is represented by a myriad of codes. These codes describe the page in a language that the computer system can read.

There are many different *page description languages,* such as Postscript, Interpress, and DDL. Unlike word processing files, it's not so easy to translate one page description language to another. A page that has been created with a page description language has to be typeset on equipment that supports the same language. The typesetter has to "speak the same language" as the page layout program.

Most of the high-quality typesetting systems that type shops currently use speak only one, if any, of these page description languages.

OBSTACLE TWO: THE DATA BASE

A type shop's most valuable asset is its data base. Each time a type shop gets a new typeface, it must add its own refinements: kerning pairs, various tracks, and so on. Those refinements come from its customers' demands, complaints, requests, and knowledge about typography, all of which go into that data base. The typesetting systems that type shops use for high-quality typesetting are designed specifically to handle that huge data base of details.

The software programs don't have that data base of typographic refinement yet. And because the page layout software and the typesetter are incompatible, your type shop can't make refinements to the job you created on your personal computer. The type shop must offer two distinct and separate services: hands-on or hands-off. You choose one or the other.

OBSTACLE THREE: WAIT AND SEE

Designers are getting a barrage of advice from computer companies, computer magazines, and computer stores about using personal computers for electronic publishing. Why do designers have to learn from people who know so little about typography?

System Incompatibility

Is it fair, then, for designers to expect direction from their type suppliers, the people who do know about type? Type shops are watching the developments in personal computers closely, and they are waiting. Waiting for better quality, faster output, compatibility between systems. But most of all they are waiting for their customers to ask for new services. As one typesetter said, "If *they* don't need it, *I* don't need it."

Right now the operators in type shops work primarily with mainframe systems. But the obstacles of incompatibility and lack of quality will soon disappear, and personal computers will be the operators' new workstations. The type shops that support customers in their exploration of new tools now are establishing a solid connection for the future.

This afternoon the salesman from the warehouse sale called me back. "There's a remote control that will work with all my different components. The only trouble is," he said, "you have to program it yourself, and it's really complicated."

I've decided to keep my toys and live with four separate remote controls for now. I'll just have to be careful about where I point them.

♦ Update: Unfortunately, we are still battling with competing standards, not only for page description languages, but also for type formats. While hardware and software manufacturers push for their choices, the users remain confused.

Consider Video

I've been playing with the buttons on the remote control that came with my new VCR. *Recall, stop, rewind, fast forward, pause* ... I can control when I watch, how fast I watch. I can start at the end, or jump to the middle. I can linger over a complicated passage or speed through a boring monologue. I can go to the beginning and start all over again. Like a video book.

I've also been studying my new television set. I opened the flap at the bottom and read the labels: VCR, disc, cable, computer, picture, color, detail, tint.... My television is actually just one piece of an information center–like the monitor for an elaborate computer graphics workstation.

I took a trip to the video store to get my membership card. It was much more crowded than the bookstore. This is the TV generation; all these people have VCRs.

Previously, I discussed the fact that you, as a designer, provide your client with more than visual direction; your expertise includes methods of production (see chapter 22, "Keeping Up with Your Clients"). Take that one step further: You must provide the most appropriate, cost-effective way to communicate with your client's client—the one we all work for—the consumer.

"I know what you're getting at," you interrupt. "You're telling me to consider all the double-income-no-kids consumers that my clients are trying to reach, and that I should consider video as a medium for visual communication. But my expertise is print, and I work with physical materials: type, photographs, illustrations."

True, you work with physical materials. But much of the production process to create those materials is not physical; instead, it consists of electronic instructions.

Here's a specific example: The major change in typesetting technology was from photographic typesetting to digital typesetting. Remember VIP? There were physical negatives of the characters, exposing light-sensitive paper or film. In digital typesetting there are no physical characters; there are instructions. When the typeface, point size, and placement are specified, the computer performs a set of instructions to produce the characters. Actual characters are not physically stored; their descriptions are.

When you design a page on a computer graphics workstation, you are working with descriptions of objects and the computer is performing your instructions. Every time you rotate, overlap, tint, stretch, move, or change the color of an object on the page, you are changing its description.

Working with electronic descriptions offers a lot of benefits. You can change an object's color or tint, stretch it, scale it, reverse it; you can add to it, subtract from it—and see all these changes without ever making it physical.

When you finally want the physical product, you have a range of choices—ink jet screen resolution for color proofs, 300-dot-per-inch laser printers for a quick black-and-white proof, 1,000-dot-per-inch plain paper typesetters for a high-resolution proof, 3,000-dot-per-inch imagesetters for a mechanical, 4,000-line 35mm film for color slides.... You have these choices because you are transmitting instructions—resolution independent, medium independent instructions—to a variety of output devices.

"OK," you concede, "I do see the value of working on a video screen to fabricate the pieces, but I still end up with physical material for the mechanical."

Not necessarily. Just as you had the option of transmitting those instructions to paper, repro, or film, you also have the option of transmitting to videotape.

Why video? You can store, or record, more than static instructions of color, typeface, point size, placement, and so on. You can also record change. The same computer graphics workstation that you use for page layout can also accommodate software for animation. Desktop publishing's counterpart is desktop video.

The medium need not be physical, and the message need not be static.

"But ..."

I know what you're going to say. You're not a video artist or an animator, and you have an appreciation for the expertise required. It's very difficult to learn all about that. Well, you're not a type designer, an illustrator, a photographer, and a writer; you are the collector and director of the various creative talents you include in your design work. Live action and animation are compatible additions to electronic visual communication.

"Wait a minute," you say. "My clients' channels of distribution are print-related. They are not television producers."

I'm not talking about broadcast television. Just as environmental design lives between print and architecture, video design lives between print and broadcast.

Picture this: Your client wants to produce a promotional guide to be used by travel agencies. The information is complex and varied: maps, transportation systems, weather charts, hotel accommodations, museum exhibits, nightclubs, and so on. He needs something that is full of life, exciting, with color and action to hold people's attention and still give them hard information. His audience is 200 people. What would you suggest?

♦ Update: Designers now take advantage of new products that can expand their vocabulary. See chapter 39, "Multimedia."

Erasing
the
Boundaries

We've all accepted the fact that computer technology is a fixed ingredient in the graphic design profession. Our acceptance is based, for the most part, on tangible, quantifiable examples of streamlined production tasks.

Once you've embraced this premise (however gingerly) to the point of working with it rather than questioning its validity, it's time to move to higher ground.

I'm not advocating that every design studio become fully computerized. I am advocating a high level of awareness. Designers make up a large proportion of the professionals who determine the form in which the consumer receives visual information; they must be aware of the forms—the methods of distribution—in which the consumer typically receives that information. Without that awareness, how can designers participate in prescribing the future of those methods?

Consider technology in graphic design on four levels:

❶ The computer as a production tool

❷ The computer as a creative tool for exploration

❸ Computer-based technology to incorporate new media

❹ Computer-based technology to design context

LEVEL ONE: REPLACEMENT TOOLS

Most designers understand the computer as a replacement tool. In your daily activities in the design studio, you can see the advantages of using word processing, accounting software, telecommunications, page layout software, charts and graphs software, and so on. You're simply replacing the traditional tools that you use for a particular production task with computer-based tools to accomplish the same tasks. This use of computers in the design environment is the obvious one.

LEVEL TWO: CREATIVE TOOLS

Now you can start to see differently and open up to new possibilities in visual forms. You have the opportunity to make mistakes, cheap mistakes—in other words, to use the tools creatively, to be innovative.

Remember when you were in school and, after reading about Moholy-Nagy, you went in the darkroom and made photograms? Do you remember spilling fixer by mistake and discovering an extraordinary shape, texture, color that you never could have preconceived? Or the first time you were left alone with a copier, and ran a black rectangle through over and over, copying the copy, enlarging it until you got a texture that resembled nothing you'd ever seen before?

A workstation that combines elements (type, photographs, line art) with functions (enlarge, combine, stretch) with characteristics (color, outline, perspective) with immediate tangible results (proof prints, repro, film) is very different from a studio with all that capacity. All those things can combine in accidental ways that don't happen when they are in different parts of the room, created at different times during the day. Speed, economy, juxtaposition, and proximity all contribute to your ability to create new textures, new typefaces, new looks, new surprises.

The computer gives you the freedom to combine real elements with unreal elements. You can light up an object with a fictitious light source. You can "map" a surface to an unlikely shape, or simulate the texture of a fabric or the shine of metal. A new tool can precipitate a new expression.

LEVEL THREE: NEW MEDIA

The next level concerns an awareness of new methods of distribution. The more you concentrate on the uses of computer technology, the more the computer itself disappears into the background; the more it takes a back seat to the issues of distribution of visual information.

In chapter 25, "Consider Video," I described the ways in which your designs could, if created in a digital medium, have the option of various output media. Elements that are stored as digital descriptions in a computer can be transmitted to paper, film, video, and so on. I talked about the new pieces of equipment that are appearing in people's homes—VCRs, CD players, sophisticated monitors—equipment with plugs and ports and labels that bear a growing resemblance to computer graphics workstations.

We as consumers have access to very sophisticated technology. Not only are we becoming comfortable with it, we are becoming indignant when it is absent. "What? No remote control? You mean I have to stand up to change the channel?" If you have a VCR and a CD player in your home, and you have no electronic tools at work, then you are, technologically speaking, a more sophisticated consumer than you are a professional. You are a *consumer* of new technology before you are a *user.*

As consumers, it is clear to us that graphic design is not limited to print, not limited to two dimensions, and not limited to being static. As graphic designers, we should see that we can design in a variety of media, and incorporate three-dimensionality and animation and (in the near future if not right now) two-way interaction.

LEVEL FOUR: DESIGNING THE CONTEXT

We need to erase boundaries.

I'm not talking about erasing boundaries between disciplines so that more graphic designers design interiors or TV shows or sign systems or sheets and pillowcases. I'm talking about the boundaries between designer, supplier, client, and consumer; the boundaries between print and video; the boundaries between problem solving and invention.

Gene Youngblood, in reference to the concept of an avant garde, called it metadesign.

Metadesign.... It's where you create context, not content. Examples are tool builders, either of hardware or software; designers of telecommunications networks; and designers of interactive videodisc systems. Each is a case of metadesign—a context, an environment is created within which further cultural production may take place. The metadesigner makes the activity possible but does not determine it. The metadesigner creates context, not content.

(Peter Broderick's interview with *Expanded Cinema* author Gene Youngblood, *Millennium Film Journal,* fall/winter 1986-87)

If we relate this specifically to graphic design on the simplest level, we think of the grid. Another level is a corporate identity program. A higher level is a design program for the client to use in his computer. A higher level still—one that places even more control in the hands of the consumer—is the interactive medium, like the interactive videodisc. Visual communication is no longer a one-way, static, fixed message. The audience—the consumer—will take a more active role in receiving information, specifically with the introduction and mass marketing of interactive videodisc technology. They will not read or watch in sequence, and will even make selections that determine the results of the information. Higher still, artificial intelligence will personalize the information for the specific viewer.

Erasing the Boundaries

We justify the cost of computers by their benefits in production. Then we make creative and visually stimulating new images. Then we begin to comprehend and utilize the various methods of distribution. And finally we erase the boundaries, incorporate metadesign, and begin to design the unpredictable, the level where the client, and even the consumer, take part in the final outcome. This level encompasses the other three.

The irony is this: the highest level—designing the context—should be the level that we study, comprehend, and evaluate first, and it should be the level in which we, as designers, actively participate.

27

Posters of the Future

The profession of graphic design, as a whole, has an attitude. We've taken a shortsighted, hands-off, I'll-do-it-if-I-have-to approach to new technology. We have problems; some are our own fault (they are self-fulfilling prophecies), and some are beyond our control.

We reject designing *for* new technology because we perceive the results as ugly. (That is because much of what we've seen hasn't been professionally designed.) We reject designing *with* new technology because computers are "too expensive. Too hard to learn. Not made for graphic designers."

We're not a target market for the hardware or software industries. We don't tend to make large capital investments. We've been labeled as reticent, a hard sell. We are neither a broad horizontal market nor a deep vertical market. In other words, if we want to participate, we'd better not wait around for an invitation.

But the biggest problem is that we don't see new technology as graphic design. This is the prelude to a huge potential loss, both for graphic designers and for new forms of visual communication.

In the previous chapter I talked about the fact that consumers—our

Posters of the Future

real clients—will have more control over the media with which they receive visual information. It's already happening. I don't have to be up by 10 A.M. to watch "Pee Wee's Playhouse"; I can record it. I don't have to sit through cornflake commercials; I can fast forward. I don't have to wait overnight for a letter; I can get a fax in seconds.

Pretty soon the consumer not only will be able to choose time and pace, but also will be able to choose content.

Let's take a look at an imaginary design job: a theater poster of the future.

What if the viewer could get a sampling—in live action—of the show itself? And what if the viewer could order the tickets by pointing to a spot on the poster?

What if your poster could be customized for each member of your audience? What if each one of that 5,000-print run could be unique? What if each poster could give several deeper levels of information, so that the viewer could find out more, such as about other events at the same theater that are of interest? Or a map that highlights the directions from his or her own house?

Designing this kind of "poster" implies an extremely complex set of problems and tasks.

A huge data base of material must be compiled, edited, composed, and recorded. Maps, photographs, text, live action, and sound all have to work together. All the links have to be considered and available: Are all viewers electronically connected to the ticket service? If not, you have to provide other instructions for getting tickets.

Each viewer's data base has to be huge, combining information about his or her own neighborhood with a larger map, so that a route can be devised from house to theater.

Finally, and most complex of all, you, as a designer, must deal with the users actually manipulating the content. What should you "lock"? How much should you let them change? What if they screw up and edit the times by mistake, or delete the poster completely?

Like two-dimensional graphic design, it all has to be assembled, designed, produced, and delivered. But the problems and tasks go many levels deeper, like a three-dimensional crossword puzzle.

This scenario is impossible today, because the technology isn't available to a large enough audience. But things change fast. It wasn't so long ago that all telephones had rotary dials.

Ten years ago, when I was at MIT, I saw a research project called Spatial Data Management System. That's a mouthful, and it's easier to describe than translate.

You're sitting in a dark room in a leather Eames chair. A video screen occupies the entire wall in front of you; it's showing you a picture of a desk, hypothetically your own. It has familiar items such as your telephone and appointment book. Next to you, at arm's length, is a small TV with the same picture. It has a touch-sensitive screen. You touch your appointment book. It opens and you see today's page, with a note about meeting a colleague at MIT's Faculty Club. Touch the words, and a map of the MIT campus appears, with the Faculty Club highlighted. A few more touches, and the map expands to include the rest of Cambridge, or farther, depending on your own location.

♦ Update: For more predictions, pick up a copy of Stewart Brand's book "The Media Lab: Inventing the Future at MIT" (Viking, 1987).

Demonstrations like this were so fragile you didn't dare breathe until the demo was over. Now many of the ideas (though much less glamorous in their presentation) are showing up on personal computers.

Many designers have consciously chosen not to work with new technology, and continue to explore other important issues in graphic design. I won't argue with that. My concern is that some designers will overlook what could be their most thought-provoking, challenging work, and that the new technology won't get the professional, experienced talent that it desperately needs.

Hot and Cold Media

My socks were still damp from the tour of the tunnels. The yellow slickers that we wore came only to my knees, and the spray from the falls made my socks wet. The theater was cool, which added to my discomfort.

The show started off slowly. I vaguely remember some story line about the first people to see Niagara Falls, but I was mostly thinking about my socks. Then the full force of a Showscan theater exploded! Seventy millimeter film, 60 frames per second, six-channel sound, and a screen that curved around my peripheral vision. The colors, the sounds, the images grabbed my senses. I was in the passenger's seat of a helicopter dropping over the edge of the falls. I felt sick. For 20 minutes I was completely immersed; nothing could distract me, wet socks included.

In September 1987, I was in San Francisco. On the second night of the AIGA conference, I went to the Exploratorium. There was a line at a small exhibit of an interactive videodisc system. I waited for my turn, and sat in front of two small video monitors and a desk that was empty except for a trackball. There was a bird's-eye view of the Golden Gate Bridge on one screen, and a cross hair over a map of the Bay Area on the other. Nothing was moving. I put my palm on the trackball and moved it to the left–the cursor moved to the left over a map of the area and I "flew" to the left of the bridge. I spun the trackball quickly and I flew faster. My concentration was intense. I was the pilot, absorbing the landscape by navigating my way over the terrain. Someone tapped me on the shoulder; the line of people waiting behind me was growing.

Mike Naimark, the creator of the videodisc, also creates environments in which the viewer is surrounded, literally, by a movie. His business card reads Environmental & Interactive Cinema.

When I got home from all of this traveling, I kept thinking about those two words: *environmental* and *interactive.* I pulled a dusty copy of Marshall McLuhan's *Understanding Media* (New York: Signet Books, 1964) off my bookshelf and opened to the chapter "Media Hot and Cold."

A hot medium is one that extends one single sense in high definition . . . the state of being well-filled with data. Hot media do not leave much to be filled in or completed by the audience. . . . Hot media are low in participation. Cool media are high in participation or completion by the audience.

My recent experiences of flying a few feet above Niagara Falls (as a passenger) and the Golden Gate Bridge (as a pilot) were contemporary versions of hot and cold media, and two extremes of the new channels through which to deliver visual communication.

The methods are familiar to designers. You want your design to attract the attention of the audience and hold it with compelling imagery. You stimulate the sense of sight by providing high-definition information.

Or you pave a smooth path for the reader, providing a logical structure for complex information. Your aim is utmost legibility, no superfluous elements. You depend upon the active participation of the reader to evaluate the content.

Or you use both compelling imagery and supportive structure.

When graphic designers talk about computers, we talk mostly about how *we* use computers. We talk about computers as production tools for graphic designers, as creative tools for graphic designers, as accounting tools for graphic designers. But that's looking at technology from one perspective. What about our audience?

Our audience doesn't care how we manufacture visual communication. They care about getting information in an effective, efficient, and hopefully enjoyable manner. With that as our task, what could be more important than understanding how people absorb visual information?

Is visual communication stronger when it's delivered in a linear, all-encompassing form, so that the judgment of the audience is suspended? Or do people absorb more information when they consciously have to make choices? Should design stimulate senses or stimulate reason? Should our audience be passive or active?

Now we have more choices with which to address these issues. On the one hand, new technology can fabricate "realities," showing us what does exist, and filling in what doesn't. Computers can fabricate light sources, surfaces, movements, textures, and environments that, like superrealist paintings, show more detail than real life shows. Environmental theaters can intensify our experiences beyond the real thing. Definitely hot.

◆ Update: New developments in interactive video are making Marshall McLuhan's insights more meaningful than ever. See chapter 40, "Interactive Media."

On the other hand, new technology will encourage people to participate actively. With no action, you'll get no *reaction*. The technology in shopping malls, airports, and two-way television lets you select your way through buildings or catalogs to find out where you need to go or what you want to buy. Businesses have data bases that instantaneously deliver whatever information is requested. Very cool.

I'm not suggesting one method over another, or that one "temperature" is a more effective way of communicating than another. But new technology offers more variety of visual experience, and that means that we have more effects to measure.

29

The Design Process

There's a restaurant in Boston on a boat moored to a dock next to the Computer Museum. One night, after a meeting of a group that uses computers in design, I overheard a discussion at the next table.

"Isn't it incredible what computers can do now? Remember when we had to use codes and type them in green monospaced characters? No mouse, no menus, no typefaces, no page layout ..."

As I listened—it was hard not to eavesdrop—I felt uncomfortable, with the same uneasiness that I'd had in the meeting. It's not that I disagreed with them; I'm as enthusiastic as they are. After a while I realized what was bothering me. Instead of comparing computers to other tools, they were comparing computers to computers.

What good are new computers if they are only better than older computers? We're interested in using computers only if they will serve us better than the tools that we are using now.

We've seen a marked improvement in the production process when we use computer tools. We can get a manuscript from a client over the telephone in a couple of minutes. We can call up a stored

The Design Process

format, pour in the text, and automatically compose a 50-page document. And so on. The production process has a predefined result. You already have the description of the piece that you intend to produce, and you proceed step-by-step to achieve that end result. The process is linear, and it's easy to articulate the steps.

But can computers improve the *design* process?

The design process is not so easy to articulate. It's not tangible; you can't point to it. The process of developing a design concept is more associative than linear. It's impossible to predict what will trigger a new idea. It is, to use a buzzword, an interactive process. You react to what you see. You create, compare, modify. When you design, you're not trying to achieve a predefined goal; you're developing something, and you discover what that something is along the way. When you're developing a concept, you have no idea of the final result. Your process is one of exploration.

Do computers enhance or inhibit the design process?

There are ingredients in the design process that are so deep, so intuitive, that they're subconscious, and we're unaware of them. Unaware, that is, until they're gone. The essential things that you rely upon—immediacy, spontaneity, portability, simultaneity—are all things we take for granted until we no longer have them.

We don't think twice about picking up a piece of repro and trying it at different angles all over the page. But when we rotate a block of type on a computer screen, we're increasingly impatient with the annoying time lag between a thought and the actual result. This year's computer may be an order of magnitude faster than last year's, but it's not as fast as the hand or the eye. If it's not instantaneous, it's not fast enough.

And then there are the external factors that interrupt the design process. Did you ever worry whether the drawing you had was compatible with your page layout? Did you ever have to refrain from using a large picture because you didn't have enough memory? Did you ever lose 14 hours of work because a piece of hardware crashed? New tools introduce new problems.

On the other hand, one of the most important ways to explore design options is to experiment, and computers are great at encouraging you to ask "What if?" "What if I use Snell Roundhand with Futura? What if I change the leading from 10 point to 14 point? What if I try a column width of 30 picas?" You can cycle through typefaces, colors, and formats without burnishing a single letter of press type, without buying a single sheet of colored paper, and without making a single phone call to the typesetter.

Let me ask you again: Do computers enhance or inhibit the design process? Is "What if?" thwarted by "Why bother?" Or do new tools infuse a creative excitement and energy that we never had with T squares, triangles, and waxers? There are so many examples of both sides. A lot depends on how you personally view the design process.

One thing is clear. Computers are in their infancy and some of us are perhaps overly impressed when, like babies, they utter their first syllable.

♦ Update: As designers gain experience with computers, they have opinions that they're eager to share. See chapter 33, "Survey Results."

But in all fairness to the dinner group that I mentioned at the beginning of this chapter, computers *are* so much better than they were five years ago; better, in some ways, than many of the tools that we use now. And they have indicated their direction clearly. They are easier to use. They are more visually oriented. They are faster. They are cheaper. The screens are bigger and have higher resolution. Computers have earned our faith, because they are moving in the right direction, and quickly. The intention is to preserve and improve the quality of the design process.

Even though we're in a difficult period, stuck with computers that are making their clumsy first steps, we are also in the unique position of being design professionals during a transition. We will have a true understanding and appreciation of tomorrow's tools because we know yesterday's and today's.

30

The
Business Side

I usually write about using computers in design and production. Lately I've been thinking a lot about how computers are used for the financial side of graphic design. In fact, most design firms buy computers for their business tasks first, for some basic reasons: to reduce repetition, to have financial information about their business readily accessible, and to use that information to make intelligent business decisions.

Every business must keep track of numbers—numbers of hours and numbers of dollars. Those of you who manually produce time sheets, status reports, utilization reports, and invoices know that there's a great deal of repetition in recording numbers and duplicating them for different sheets, reports, folders, and logbooks.

You need the numbers for more than writing checks and sending invoices. You need to look at those numbers in various configurations, and you need them quickly.

Say a client calls and asks how much he's spent so far and what's left in both hours and money. Or you're bidding on a complex job, and you need to make intelligent estimates based on past experience. Your ability to have a different configuration of information at any moment is limited by the time it would take you to get it.

One kind of program often used in computer-aided business is a data base. A data base is an organized collection of information: the contents and the structure. Think of your file cabinets, full of papers (like time sheets, project expenses, and so on) that are placed in their appropriate files and hanging folders.

As in a manual system, there are relationships among the various files in a data base program. When a client calls and asks for a lot of numbers, you simply call up the client's record and ask the computer to show you all related records. The computer will show you the current totals based on the most recent information you entered. The computer can also sort—that is, rank the records in order, so you could, for example, list clients in the order of who owed you the most money.

Clifford Selbert Design has recently automated its accounting and project tracking and billing with a software package called Adman. Cliff says the company's business was like NASA; over the years NASA has collected buildings full of data—samples, numbers, photographs—and has examined only 1 percent of it for analysis. That's what was happening in his firm: Numbers that could reveal important facts about his business were in cold storage.

Now, in addition to automating its manual system, CSD is making better use of its numbers to make decisions about its future, such as when to hire new people, what projects it can take on as pro bono work, and so on.

When you consider using a data base, there's a basic decision to make: You can buy a prepackaged data base, or you can start from scratch.

The first option is a data base program that has already been designed for your type of application. It's like getting the cabinets and files and folders with all the tags and drawers labeled and all the relationships defined; you're told exactly what you need and where to put everything. They give you the base; you just fill in the data. There are a number of programs on the market, for advertising agencies or design firms, that are like the one CSD chose.

The Business Side

Or you can buy a data base program that provides tools for you to define and set up the structure and relationships. At WGBH Educational Foundation, the design department decided to automate its billing, utilization reports, and status reports. It couldn't buy a prepackaged program because of its own complexity and because it had to adhere to WGBH's established accounting system. Daniele Skopek, financial analyst for the department, hired a programmer, and over the course of six months they designed, programmed, and implemented their automated system.

If you buy a packaged system, don't expect it to be perfect—no generic system can cover the idiosyncrasies of your particular company. And a package is difficult, if not impossible, to alter. On the other hand, if you design the data base, you must model it on a well-defined manual system, and even then you can't possibly predict everything. At WGBH, reports could take as long as three hours to process. That, along with several other problems, prompted them to reevaluate and redesign the system. Now anyone can get a report in minutes.

I hardly need to say this, but I can't leave it out either: A computer will not tell you what the numbers mean. It is only a tool that will give you the information you need. It will not transform your bookkeeper into a financial analyst. Any tool is useless—even dangerous—in the wrong hands. Choosing and using a good system requires the participation of experts in design, finance, and computers.

But one thing is clear: There are a lot of numbers that hold a lot of secrets waiting to be revealed.

31

·········

Design Tools

Some designers say that they won't touch computers because they hate the computer "look." The funny thing is, much of the work that is designed and produced using computers shows no physical signs of the computer. Some of the best work you see may have been conceived with a mouse instead of a marker. The factors that do change—the costs, the speed, the efficiency with which the work was created—are invisible in the design itself, but they are clearly evident in the proposal and the invoice to the client.

I've been seeing Ronn Campisi's work for two decades—I saw it weekly when he was art director at the *Real Paper,* monthly when he was art director at *Boston Magazine,* and daily when he was art director at the *Boston Globe.*

Somewhere during the latter part of those years, Ronn started using computers. When he opened his studio, Ronn Campisi Design, he immediately equipped his office with a personal computer and a laser printer.

The look of his designs has not changed since the time he used traditional tools. The change is in the amount of time and money he spends to produce his publication design prototypes, and the service he provides his clients. There, the change is radical. He has provided them with faster turnaround time, lower typesetting costs, a better method of type specification, and additional advice

Design Tools

in production using computers. He is very particular, and will not use something of low quality. He is also conscientious about prices, and will not charge a client $14,000 for typesetting when he knows that the job can be produced for under $3,000.

Ronn has developed a repertoire of tools and materials for the work in which he specializes: publication design. His studio is an appropriate blend of traditional and new procedures, materials, and tools:

Hardware: Macintosh II; 40-megabyte hard disk; Super Mac color monitor; Super Mac Spectrum video card; 1-megabyte memory (more on order); extended keyboard.

Macintosh Plus; 20-megabyte hard disk

LaserWriter Plus

Canon copier

Kroy color machine

Software: PageMaker 3.0; Microsoft Word. plus over 100 fonts, all the pads and markers and paper you'd expect to find in a traditional studio, and as much computer memory as he can get his hands on.

▶Using page layout software, Ronn Campisi tries a layout and prints it out on his laser printer. Then he uses a color transfer machine to get color type and line art, and cuts out sample photos from magazines.

Photograph © 1988 Peter Jones.

For a typical comp of a prototype page, Ronn has determined the page size, the basic grid, the margins, and the type styles that he plans to use before he sits down at the computer. Then he sets up the underlying grid and, using a page layout program, lays out the copy and headlines on the page, tries several different layouts, and prints them out on the laser printer. Sometimes he prints out the page on transparent paper, and colors the back with magic marker.

Ronn gives each element's specifications a name or a code. When several elements always appear together, he gives that list of specs—which includes type and relationships—one name. Basically, he's creating master style sheets.

Later, when laying out pages, he applies the specification names to the appropriate manuscript text. The text appears on the screen with the specified typography. If he has to change the specs for a particular element, or simply wants to try it, he changes the master

▶Ronn gives each element's specification a code. This is a master style sheet.

THE MAINE TIMES 13

Ronn Campisi Design

Comments
Movies

COMMENTS

▲▲▲▲▲▲▲▲▲▲▲▲▲▲▲▲▲▲▲▲▲▲▲▲

Movies: Masquerade...Raising Maine: Skating through life...Food: Eat your way through New England...Gardening: Old-time farmers... Dance: Natural performing

sp11
cm.slg — MOVIES

One line space of style **cm.slg**

hd30fl
sp22
Hairline rules

Shock, schlock, and the old black magic

tl —— **The Serpent and the Rainbow**
Directed by Wes Craven
inf —— *Written by Richard Maxwell and A.R. Simoun*
Starring Bill Pullman, Cathy Tyson, and Zakes Mokae

One line space of **tx**

txf —— **D**RUMS PULSE in the Caribbean night. Shadows shift at the edge of vision—forms (animal? human? supernatural?) stirring against dense foliage . . . Oh, sure, they were corny

bl2 —— *—by Robert McKibben*

• *The L-shaped hairline rules are in the PageMaker template pasteboard.*

Design Tools

COMMENTS

▲▲▲▲▲▲▲▲▲▲▲▲▲▲▲▲▲▲▲▲▲▲▲

Movies: Indiana Jones and the Last Crusade — slick tour de force...Visual Arts: Michael Reece — influence and anxiety...Eating Out: Christopher's: Greek with gusto...Music: 900-year-old family tradition...Gardening: Battling bugs

. . . .

THE WEATHER REPORT

Mosquitoes, gray skies, and flannel sheets

"IT'S BEEN rain forest weather," Steve Yates said. Indeed. Rainfall last week was seldom under two inches, and the Miners recorded more than five inches on Cape Rosier. It's a stark contrast to last summer's beginnings, when everyone was talking drought. If anything, we have almost too much precipitation. Steve tried to be cheerful, though. "After all, this is Maine," he said. "The pattern will probably change soon and we'll go six weeks without any rain at all."

Penobscot Bay

Margaret Vaughan was eating fresh lettuce all week from her garden. The carrots and beans were up, too. "A lot of people haven't even planted yet," she said. "It's been so wet they haven't had a chance." Olive-backed, hermit, and wood thrushes were singing in the trees near the house. And the mosquitoes and black

mosquitoes in mind, and only the cool mornings late in the week provided any respite. Sunday's breezes were nice, in places where they could be felt. I was working in the open garage and had to endure swarms of the critters to get anything accomplished.

In the Sky

"This is the week Mainers can rejoice and get serious about summer," proclaimed Alan Davenport at the University of Maine planetarium in Orono. The sun declares the official beginning of summer Wednesday by climbing to its maximum altitude. The summer solstice occurs at 5:44 a.m., and in Maine that means the sun will reach a noontime height of almost 70 degrees above the southern horizon and the day will be 15 hours and 37 minutes long.

The full moon, in contrast, will hang

▶The Maine Times's production department uses the specs directly from Ronn's disk. The page is set with all pieces in place, except the photo.

spec. All text that has that name will change automatically throughout the pages of the publication.

Those electronic specifications are also descriptions for his laser printer or a compatible high-resolution typesetter. If the client's production department is using equipment and software that is compatible with Ronn's, it uses the specs directly from Ronn's disk. In fact, Ronn often advises clients on the software that they should use so that they can take full advantage of electronic specifications.

An important outcome of electronic specifications is the documentation that Ronn supplies for his clients. Before he used computers, his documentation of type specs were photocopies of sample text, with his specs hand-written. Now Ronn simply prints out sample pages and indicates the specification names or codes that his clients should use when typesetting their publication. For his clients who do own or use compatible equipment, his hard-copy documentation is a reference guide only; the guidelines can be transferred in electronic form. The guidelines are basically "living specifications."

Studios that take advantage of new tools do so with choice. For much design work, traditional tools may be superior to computer-based tools and materials. If an INT is more accurate than an ink jet print, then that is the method of choice. If a typeface is available on a laser printer, it is clearly more cost-effective for comps than traditional typesetting. I don't know any designers who want their work to look as if it was designed and produced using a computer. But I do know a lot of designers who want to provide the best work in the most cost-effective manner.

Furthermore, it's essential that your tools are chosen for the work that you do. A design firm that specializes in environmental graphics will not have the same tools and materials as one that specializes in annual reports.

Finally, whether you own the technology, or you hire an outside service that owns the technology, or your client owns the technology, the bottom line is this: If your firm or department is not aware of the radical changes that computers have introduced to your profession, you cannot possibly offer your clients the full expertise they deserve.

◆ Update: That was 1988. It's now impossible to keep up with Ronn's purchases. His studio has more up-to-date software than most computer stores.

The rest of the tools and materials that he uses to produce the comp have nothing to do with personal computers. They include a copier, a color transfer machine, magic markers, Letratone, sample photos from magazines, and Pantone sheets. The separate elements are cut and pasted, then copied on a color laser copier (at a local copy center) to create a single sheet for presentation.

Ronn watches constantly for tools that will allow him to work faster, with more fluidity, playfulness, and flexibility to make changes. He also watches for tools that will streamline the tasks for producing and documenting the type specifications and the guidelines for the layout.

Ronn's primary need for the computer is access to type—to have it immediately, to have it cheaply, to have it any size, and to have its specifications stored electronically.

Design
Technology
Survey

During the spring of 1988, Dick Coyne
and I had an ongoing telephone conversation. What are designers
buying? What are they using computers for? Dick finally said, "Maybe
we should do a survey in the magazine and publish the results." I
was so excited by the idea that I wrote the survey immediately, and
we put it in the next issue. The survey had this opening paragraph:

*Creative professionals are eager to know what their colleagues are doing
with computers. We're asking you to complete this survey so that we can provide
you with that information. Fill in your answers, tear out the page, fold it,
tape it closed, and mail it no later than June 10, 1988. If your answers
need more room than the space provided, you can tape an extra sheet inside.
If you have work that you produced with the aid of computers and would like
to share it, please send slides in a separate envelope and a brief description of
the computer system you used.*

Design and Technology

▶Readers were asked to fill out this survey form in the spring of 1988.

Name _____ Title _____

Company _____

Address _____ City _____ State ____ Zip _____

DON'T OWN COMPUTERS

1. *Please check your primary business:*
☐ graphic design   ☐ illustration
☐ photography   ☐ advertising
☐ other

2. *How many people are in your studio/department?* _____

3. *Do you plan to buy computers?*
☐ yes   ☐ no   ☐ don't know

4. *If so, what kind and how many of each?*
Please list model or system name.
Apple _____
IBM or compatible _____
other _____
☐ don't know

5. *What software products do you plan to use?*
_____
_____
_____
☐ don't know

6. *How much do you plan to spend?*
☐ 0   ☐ $50,000-$100,000
☐ under $5,000   ☐ over $100,000
☐ $5,000-$20,000   ☐ don't know
☐ $20,000-$50,000

7. *Do you use computer service bureaus?*
☐ yes   ☐ no

8. *Do your clients ask you to use computers in your work?*
☐ yes   ☐ no

9. *If so, for what purpose?*
_____
_____
_____

10. *Why do you want to buy computers?*
_____
_____
_____

11. *Why don't you want to buy computers?*
_____
_____
_____

12. *Why haven't you bought a computer yet?*
_____
_____
_____

Design Technology Survey

DO OWN COMPUTERS

1. *Please check your primary business:*
☐ graphic design ☐ illustration
☐ photography ☐ advertising
☐ other

2. *How many people are in your studio/department?* _____

3. *What kind of computers and how many of each?*
Please list model or system name.
Apple _____
IBM or compatible _____
other _____

4. *What software products do you use?*
_____
_____
_____

5. *How much has your studio/department spent on software and computer-related equipment?* _____

6. *How much do you plan to spend on computers next year?* _____

7. *In what area of your work are computers used the most?*
☐ production ☐ business
☐ design ☐ other

8. *For which categories do you use your computers?*
☐ 2-D print ☐ video
☐ packaging ☐ industrial design
☐ slides ☐ ad layout
☐ environmental design ☐ other

9. *How many of the people in your studio/department use the computers?* _____

10. *Do your clients ask you to use computers in your work?*
☐ yes ☐ no

11. *If so, for what purpose?*
_____
_____
_____

12. *Have you changed the way in which you bill clients?*
☐ yes ☐ no

13. *If so, how?* _____
_____
_____
_____

14. *What is the biggest problem you've experienced with the use of computers?* _____
_____
_____
_____

15. *What is the biggest benefit?*
_____
_____
_____

16. *Overall, do you feel that computers have a positive or negative effect on your work?*
☐ positive ☐ negative

Survey Results

During the summer of 1988, Dick and Patrick Coyne periodically bundled and sent the survey results to my office in Cambridge, where we entered the information in our data base. We were delighted with the responses; they provide an excellent representation of what designers, photographers, illustrators, and other graphic arts professionals are doing with computers.

We listed the responses to each question as percentages. By using the data base program, we were also able to ask multiple questions such as "What percentage of design studios with only one designer spent over $20,000?" Many of the respondents had additional comments, which we included.

There's an interesting trend that shows up in the charts at the end of this chapter: In many cases, small studios are spending approximately the same amount as large studios. Think of this compared to the vast differences between the totals that small and large studios spend on space, telephone services, salaries, employee benefits, and so on.

Survey Results

Don't Own Computers

30% of you do not own computers.

1. *Please check your primary business:*
- 76% graphic design
- 6% photography
- 11% illustration
- 15% advertising
- 1% publisher
- 11% other

As you will see above and in many cases, the totals are higher than 100% because respondents selected more than one answer.

2. *How many people are in your studio/department?*
- 35% 1 person
- 21% 2 people
- 10% 3 people
- 11% 4 people
- 8% 5 people
- 9% 6-10 people (inclusive)
- 5% 11-20 (inclusive)
- 1% more than 20 people

3. *Do you plan to buy computers?*
- 79% yes
- 10% no
- 10% don't know
- 1% no answer

4. *If so, what kind and how many of each? Please list model or system name.*
- 23% Apple
- 2% MacPlus
- 10% Mac SE
- 21% Mac II
- 10% IBM or compatible
- 2% other
- 24% don't know
- 8% no answer

As you can see, some respondents simply said Apple, and some specified the model. Altogether, 56% plan to buy Apple computers.

5. *What software products do you plan to use?*
- 11% business
- 8% paint
- 4% word processing
- 4% page
- 26% PageMaker
- 25% Illustrator
- 9% Microsoft Word
- 8% MacDraw
- 4% Xpress
- 4% FreeHand
- 3% ReadySetGo!
- 2% MacWrite
- 13% other
- 27% don't know
- 16% no answer

Some respondents answered with a category of software; most answered with specific product names.

6. *How much do you plan to spend?*
- 3% 0
- 25% under $5,000
- 46% $5,000-$20,000
- 4% $20,000-$50,000
- 3% $50,000-$100,000
- 0 over $100,000
- 19% don't know

7. *Do you use computer service bureaus?*
- 12% yes
- 84% no
- 4% no answer

8. *Do your clients ask you to use computers in your work?*
- 29% yes
- 68% no
- 3% no answer

9. *If so, for what purpose?*

- 19% design
- 19% production
- 2% business
- 2% illustration
- 10% other
- 68% no answer

10. *Why do you want to buy computers?*

- 35% increase productivity
- 22% time
- 21% keep up with the trade
- 6% typesetting
- 5% keep up with clients
- 5% new ideas
- 3% quality
- 3% production
- 3% cost savings
- 10% other

11. *Why don't you want to buy computers?*

12. *Why haven't you bought a computer yet?*

We found that almost all respondents felt that this was essentially the same question, so we combined the answers:

- 44% cost
- 17% lack of knowledge
- 8% staff and/or boss resistance
- 8% product limitations
- 8% don't like computers
- 3% equipment is changing
- 3% time
- 1% fear
- 23% other
- 8% no answer

Do Own Computers

70% of you do own computers.

1. *Please check your primary business:*

- 68% graphic design
- 6% photography
- 7% illustration
- 15% advertising
- 3% publishing
- 18% other

2. *How many people are in your studio/department?*

- 17% 1 person
- 21% 2 people
- 15% 3 people
- 10% 4 people
- 6% 5 people
- 17% 6-10 people (inclusive)
- 10% 11-20 (inclusive)
- 4% more than 20 people

3. *What kind of computers and how many of each? Please list model or system name.*

- 10% Apple
- 14% MacPlus
- 18% Mac SE
- 17% Mac II
- 2% Apple IIE
- 22% IBM or compatible
- 2% IBM XT
- 1% IBM AT
- 12% other

Many respondents own several different kinds of computers, or several of the same kind of computer. As in the "don't own" section, some listed the product's company name, and some listed the actual model.

Survey Results

4. *What software products do you use?*

- 10% paint
- 2% word processing
- 4% page layout
- 2% business
- 56% PageMaker
- 38% Microsoft Word
- 34% Illustrator
- 18% MacDraw
- 14% FreeHand
- 14% SuperPaint
- 14% Excel
- 14% CricketDraw
- 12% Xpress
- 11% MacWrite
- 8% HyperCard
- 7% Ventura
- 6% ReadySetGo!
- 5% Lotus
- 2% fonts*
- 58% other

Again the total is higher than 100%, because most respondents own more than one software package.

As in "don't own," some answered with product categories, and most answered with specific product names. If a product was named fewer than four times, we placed it in the "other" category. The "other" category is extremely high, and this is not surprising. There are so many software packages out there!

*This is an unrealistic number because we assume that many respondents don't think of fonts as software, and so did not list them.

5. *How much has your studio/department spent on software and computer-related equipment?*

- 1% under $500
- 2% $500-$1,000
- 4% $1,000-$2,500
- 11% $2,500-$5,000
- 20% $5,000-$10,000
- 25% $10,000-$20,000
- 14% $20,000-$50,000
- 5% $50,000-$100,000
- 6% over $100,000
- 12% no answer

6. *How much do you plan to spend on computers next year?*

- 8% under $500
- 6% $500-$1,000
- 10% $1,000-$2,500
- 16% $2,500-$5,000
- 16% $5,000-$10,000
- 9% $10,000-$20,000
- 7% $20,000-$50,000
- 3% $50,000-$100,000
- 1% over $100,000
- 24% no answer

7. *In what area of your work are computers used the most?*

- 62% production
- 58% design
- 48% business
- 9% other

8. *For which design categories do you use your computers?*

- 69% 2-D print
- 17% packaging
- 25% slides
- 9% environmental design
- 10% video
- 6% industrial design
- 56% ad layout
- 11% word processing
- 12% other

Again, the totals are higher than 100% because respondents selected more than one answer.

9. *How many of the people in your studio/department use the computers?*
The following percentages should be read as, for example, "In the studios/departments that have four people, an average of 80% of the people use the computers." Keep in mind that the answers for this question can be misleading; you might conclude that in large companies fewer people use computers, but it's more likely that there are not enough computers to go around.

- 98% 1 person*
- 90% 2 people
- 80% 3 people
- 80% 4 people
- 81% 5 people
- 66% 6-10 people
- 58% 11-20 people
- 59% over 20 people

*In other words, a few respondents who have one-person studios or departments have a computer but don't use it.

10. *Do your clients ask you to use computers in your work?*
- 51% yes
- 43% no
- 6% no answer

11. *If so, for what purpose?*
- 36% production
- 33% design
- 1% word processing
- 5% other
- 50% no answer

12. *Have you changed the way in which you bill clients?*
- 35% yes
- 52% no
- 13% no answer

13. *If so, how?*
- 8% computer time
- 1% laser printouts
- 23% other
- 68% no answer

There was a great deal of variety in the "other" answers. Some respondents interpreted the question in terms of using a computer for creating invoices; others answered in terms of rates.

14. *What is the biggest problem you've experienced with the use of computers?*
- 18% learning curve
- 17% program limitations
- 9% time
- 8% incompatibility
- 7% training
- 5% keeping up with technology
- 4% support
- 4% need more computers
- 3% quality
- 3% cost
- 2% staff problems
- 2% acceptance
- 1% manuals
- 7% other

15. *What is the biggest benefit?*
- 47% time
- 8% easy changes in design
- 7% production ease
- 7% cost
- 6% control
- 4% creativity
- 4% freedom
- 2% quality
- 8% other

16. *Overall, do you feel that computers have a positive or negative effect on your work?*
- 93% positive
- 1% negative
- 6% don't know

Survey Results

Along with your multiple-choice answers, many of you gave us enlightening and thoughtful comments about the problems and benefits of using computers. We'd like to quote some of the comments–both positive and negative.

CHANGES IN BILLING

"Changes in billing clients went from hourly rates to flat rates."
"Higher hourly rate from combining design and production."
"Billing changed from per unit for artwork to hourly."
"Hourly rate increased because less time is used."
"New labor categories–billing computer time rather than typesetting and layout."
"Fewer out-of-pocket expenses."
"Sometimes bill for computer time plus operator time."
"Planning to increase hourly rate as we become more proficient."
"More project oriented, less hourly."
"Added an additional charge per hour to cover equipment costs. This works out because of time savings with computer."
"Hourly rate adjusted lower, type costs reduced."
(I find the comments above frightening. Clients are already confused enough about design fees.)

THE PROBLEMS

"Addiction. The money pit. Constant need for more: more memory, more programs, more storage . . ."
"Biggest problem is overcoming bugs on tight deadlines."
"Not enough courses that are relevant to design."
"Lack of links from design to production."
"Not enough workstations for everyone."
"Lack of compatibility with existing typesetting systems."
"Bad manuals."
"Learning-curve frustration."
"Client or management people think the job can be done quicker/cheaper."
"It's very difficult to educate the client in capabilities and weaknesses."

"Limited typeface selection."

"Having to learn limitations not mentioned by salespeople."

"Trying to make (computers) a solve-all tool."

"New users skip over basics and don't keep good files."

"Vaporware."

"Helplessness when technical problems occur."

"The technology is not advanced enough in color and image."

"Clients send layouts via modem." (Is this a benefit or a problem?)

"Clients think they are designers just because they have software packages."

"Spending lots of time fine-tuning, noodling till it's perfect."

"Poor service and support from dealers."

"Real situations are more complex than the ads lead you to believe."

"Major restructuring of job duties."

"Proofreading is now my responsibility, not the typesetter's. Copy input is a pain."

"Keeping up."

"Losing data."

"Being on the bleeding edge of technology can be painful."

BENEFITS

"Ability to forecast business."

"Reduced dependence, increased control and flexibility and autonomy; I don't have to hire support staff."

"Use it in billing clients—helps me to track expenses."

"Have spent about one year's salary of an assistant on computers." (This is a benefit when you read the next two comments.)

"Can do the work of two."

"I can do the work of 10 people."

"Freedom to experiment."

"Using information supplied on disk."

"Ability to do self-promotional mailings."

"I'm getting more software and hardware companies for clients."

"Immediacy: don't have to go to the stat camera."

"It's the 'in' thing."

Survey Results

"Freedom from suppliers."
"Increased professional perception from clients."
"Good preparation for future computer applications."
"Saving clients' money."
"Time savings."
"Modifying type."
"High-quality comps, proposals."
"Speed and superior control over design because changes are so easy."
"Cheaper than conventional typesetting."
"Self-sufficiency as a one-person business. And I can be competitive price-wise with the big agencies."
"Higher quality per budget dollar on any given project."
"Meeting with other graphic designers to share information and experiences."
"It's FUN!!"

When you read the comments and consider the vast amounts of time, money, and brain cells spent on computers, you might wonder, "Is it worth it?"

Well, remember the last question for the "Do Owns" on our survey: "Overall, do you feel that computers have a positive or negative effect on your work?" The results:

- 93% positive

- 1% negative

- 6% don't know

Numbers like those are convincing. Couple them with a powerful remark in the *AIGA Journal* by Edward Tufte: "Probably the best evidence for making the transition is that few people have ever gone back to the typewriter and ruling pen once they've gotten a competent personal computer system."

Design and Technology

THOSE WHO DON'T OWN: DOLLARS YOU PLAN TO SPEND

Number of
People in the
Studio

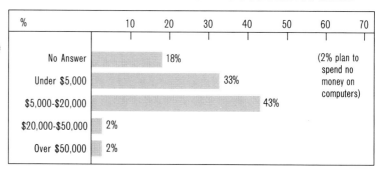

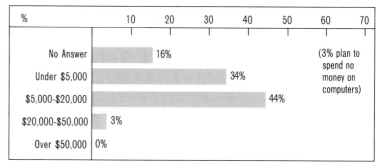

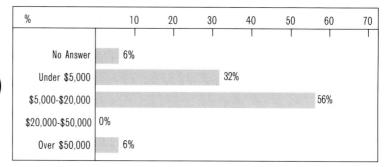

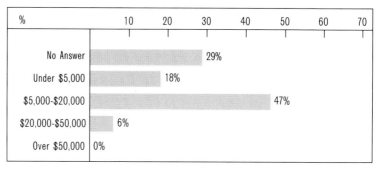

Survey Results

Number of People in the Studio

5

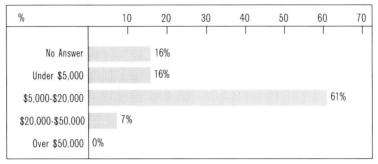

6-10

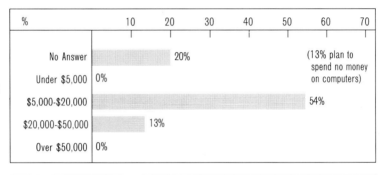

11-20

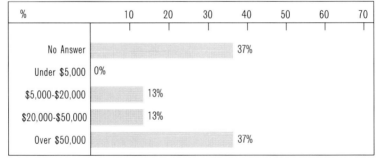

Design and Technology

THOSE WHO OWN: DOLLARS YOU'VE ALREADY SPENT

Number of
People in the
Studio

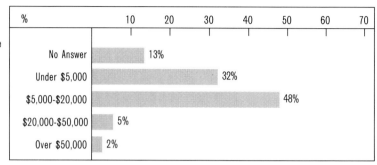

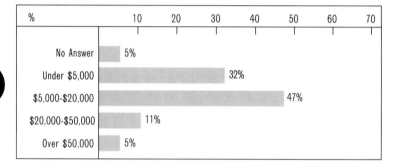

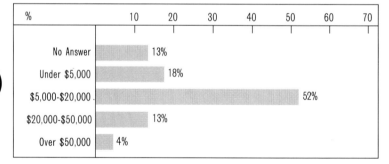

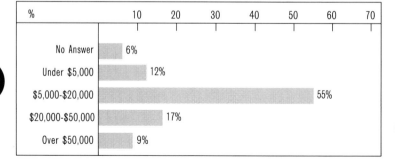

Survey Results

Number of People in the Studio

5

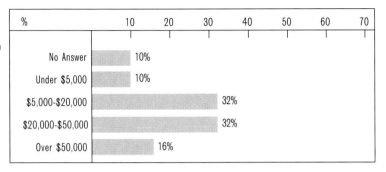

6-10

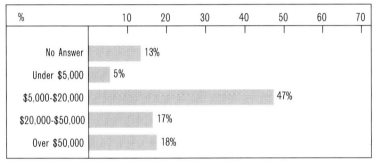

11-20

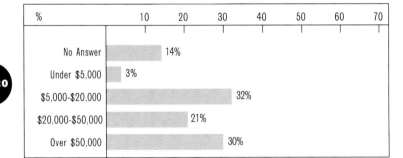

21+

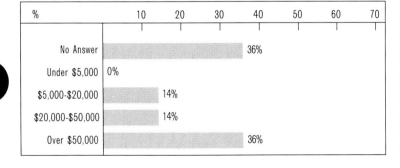

Design and Technology

THOSE WHO OWN: DOLLARS YOU PLAN TO SPEND

Number of
People in the
Studio

1

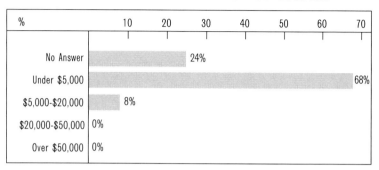

No Answer	24%
Under $5,000	68%
$5,000-$20,000	8%
$20,000-$50,000	0%
Over $50,000	0%

2

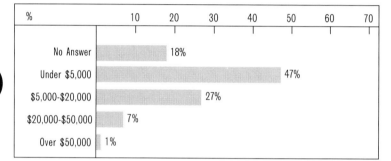

No Answer	18%
Under $5,000	47%
$5,000-$20,000	27%
$20,000-$50,000	7%
Over $50,000	1%

3

No Answer	31%
Under $5,000	40%
$5,000-$20,000	27%
$20,000-$50,000	2%
Over $50,000	0%

4

No Answer	21%
Under $5,000	47%
$5,000-$20,000	29%
$20,000-$50,000	3%
Over $50,000	0%

Survey Results

Number of People in the Studio

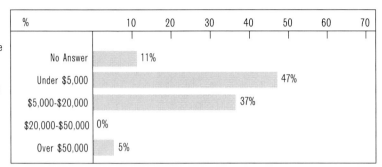

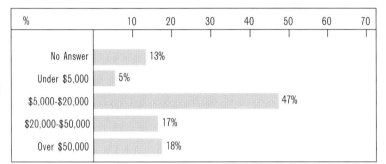

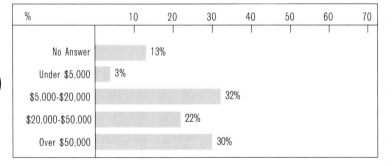

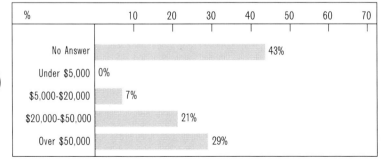

34

·········

Poor Shopping

During the fall of 1988, I read, tabulated, and published the findings from our Design Technology Survey. I also spent a great deal of time talking with designers about their computer purchases. Now, rather than reporting the facts, I'd like to tell you what I think about your buying habits.

You idiots!

You're in a profession that has always been known for spending very little on equipment. You could start a design studio with a telephone and a drawing board. A copier was a major purchase. And the research that you did before you bought that copier was exhaustive. You knew it inside out before you signed a leasing agreement, let alone before paying the full amount.

All of a sudden you're writing checks for $15,000 in equipment before you even know what you're going to do with it. I'm the last person to tell you not to buy computers. There's no question that computers are and will be an integral part of your work. But you are buying blindly, and you are buying backward. As a result, you're spending more money more rapidly than you need to.

You are walking into stores and asking salespeople what you should buy. First of all, they don't know your business. They probably know little about graphic design. Their job is to sell.

Go ahead, listen to the salesperson and buy everything you might ever need right now, and then you can have $15,000 sitting on a table taking up space instead of sitting in your bank account. For that matter, why not hire a new employee you don't need and have that person sit at a desk for eight months until you figure out what to do with him or her? You may think that's absurd, but you have no idea how many people call me and say, "I just spent $15,000 for equipment. Now I have to figure out what to do with it."

For many of you, your buying is motivated by fear. You're afraid that you will be left behind. You will lose clients.

And guilt. You know you should be studying, learning, researching the subject. But it's time-consuming just to find help, let alone do the research yourself. And when you go to a store, it's confusing, irrelevant, and often wholly unappetizing. So by spending 15 grand you figure you can assuage your guilt and feel comfortable knowing that you, too, have a state-of-the-art design studio.

Or you see that your employees are looking enviously at other studios that have computers. You feel guilty, and fearful that you will lose your valued employees. So you go out and buy equipment. I'll tell you what should make you feel *really* guilty and scared: You buy the stuff, but you don't allow your employees the time or pay for the guidance to learn how to use it. No one has any time to learn anything other than to write memos with the equipment. You're stingy with your billable hours, and yet you spend $15,000. So now you have a $15,000 typewriter.

Don't interpret my words as telling you not to buy computers. You have no choice but to buy and use computers. If you fail, you *will* be left behind, and you *will* lose clients, and your employees *will* quit. But you should know what you're buying and why you're buying.

I've combined several real-life scenarios into one and invented a fictitious name to protect the guilty. Here's how it goes.

A designer calls me and introduces himself as Max. Max tells me he's going to buy the whole nine yards. He wants to know what I think. I say, "Wait a minute, let's back up. What are you planning on using this setup for?"

"So that I can be more productive."

"How do you plan to be more productive?"

"By saving time."

"And how will you save time?"

"By having computers."

He's been watching too many commercials on TV.

He reads me his shopping list that he has filled in with the help of a salesperson.

"A Mac II with 80 megabits of RAM and 5 megabits internal."

I say, "You mean 5 megabytes of RAM and an 80-megabyte internal hard disk."

"Yeah, right."

"Why did you buy so much memory?"

"Well, better safe than sorry."

He continues, "A LaserWriter printer and a scanner."

I ask, "How many gray levels does the scanner have?"

"I don't know."

"Do you know how many gray levels you need?"

"No."

"Why did you choose this one?"

"The salesperson told me it was top of the line, and as a designer, I need the best quality."

(This is my pet peeve. No desktop scanner is going to give you the quality you really need for high-quality reproduction, and in many cases you're better off with the low end if using the scanner for comps and templates.)

"OK," I say, "go on."

"A tape backup," says Max.

"First learn to back up on floppies. When you have so many files that backing up on floppies becomes a real pain, then you'll know why you need a tape backup and you'll have an intelligent reason for buying it."

The list continues.

"And we're buying an ImageWriter."

"Why are you buying an ImageWriter when you're already buying a laser printer?"

Poor Shopping

"Because of that neat effect you get from those blocky edges."

"April Greiman may be doing great things with pixels, but please. There are better ways to get poor-quality effects than spending an extra $600!"

This was the clincher. Max says, "And I'm buying OCR software."

"Do you know what OCR software is?"

"No, but it's only $400, and compared to everything else I'm buying, that's cheap."

Bit by bit (so to speak), we hack away at the shopping list and remove about $6,000.

Max may well eventually need those extras. But for God's sake, he shouldn't buy something before he even knows what he's going to do with it! So I tell Max, "You must know what your essentials are. I promise you, when you come back next month to buy more equipment, the salesperson won't tell you to take your money someplace else. But for now, Max, leave that money in the bank!"

◆ Update: The earlier shopping suggestions are as valid as ever. See chapter 19, "Varied Tasks," and chapter 20, "A Dedicated System."

35

Commission a Typeface

I have talked a lot about how designers are using computers. I have talked about computers as tools that replace our old tools, like the triangle and the T square, and as creative tools that let us experiment and develop new looks, new surprises.

In each case the designer is using the computer. Hands-on.

But much of a designer's work is not in actually creating pieces; the work is in collecting and orchestrating the pieces. Your project involves a team of talent, which may include a photographer, an illustrator, and a copywriter.

You also bring a type designer to the team. Chances are, though, you'll never meet him. He's probably dead. But even the type designers who are very much alive and well and producing typefaces that we use daily are quite remote to us. Would you ever telephone a type designer and say, "Hey, I've got a job to design a brochure, and I've got my photographer and my copywriter. How would you like to design the typeface?" Probably not.

Well, think twice. The technological revolution that brought publishing to the desktop has also brought type design and production to the desktop. If you are one of the many designers who uses a

Commission a Typeface

Macintosh computer to spec type and set pages, you have an opportunity that otherwise would not have been within your reach.

You can commission a typeface.

The hardware and software necessary to create electronic pages has made its way to our studios. A Macintosh with page layout, drawing, and image-manipulation programs doesn't have the power and sophistication of the high-end systems like Scitex, but for the comparative price tag, it does the job.

The same is true of the systems that are used to create digital type masters. Off-the-shelf software programs such as Altsys Fontographer do not have the sophistication of a full-blown system used at digital type foundries such as Bitstream Inc. (see chapter 2, "Digital Type Masters"). But when they are placed in the hands of talented type designers, beautiful letterforms can be produced.

My introduction to this new idea came from Roger Black and David Berlow. As art director of such magazines as *Rolling Stone* and *Newsweek,* Roger has been in the position of commissioning typefaces, as he did for those two magazines. Over the past couple of years, Roger has brought desktop technology to his publication design work, and he definitely pushes the envelope. When Roger designed the new magazine *Smart,* he contacted David Berlow, one of the original type designers at Bitstream Inc. Using Fontographer, David produced a revival of Lucian Bernhard's 1920s design, Lucian. David is taking it another step and has designed an original italic version, which should appear in the next issue of *Smart.*

Why not share a good thing and make money to boot? The new service is called The Font Bureau, and if you supply the original artwork, it will create a PostScript font in Macintosh format. As of this writing, fees start at $2,500, or about the price of several days'

►When Roger Black designed the new magazine "Smart," he commissioned David Berlow to produce a revival of the typeface Lucian.

time of a professional photographer. Most fonts can be completed 30 days after the receipt of your artwork. If it's a type revival that requires extensive research and development, the fee is about $5,000. Believe me, you will have access to some of the richest minds of typographic knowledge around. For more information, contact The Font Bureau at 80 Fifth Avenue, New York, New York 10011, (212) 727-2770.

There are a number of talented independent type designers who have been designing fonts—revivals and originals—for the Macintosh for years. Peter Fraterdeus not only designs type for the Macintosh and PostScript output devices; he also publishes a typographic newsletter called *Mice Type*. A beautiful font of his that attracted my attention is called MIA Prospera. You can contact Peter at Alphabets, Inc., 804 Dempster Street, Evanston, Illinois 60202, (312) 328-2733.

Another designer to watch is Joe Treacy of Treacyfaces Inc. Joe has designed many logos using Fontographer and Illustrator, and by the time you read this, you will be able to buy his original typefaces for your Macintosh. You may also commission a full typeface or a subset. Joe mentioned a detail that will be a major creative tool for designers: His faces will include an Illustrator-compatible version with the typeface package, so that you can have access to the character's control points along its outline. That means you can manipulate the character's shape, perhaps to create a logo. Treacyfaces is located at 111 Sibley Avenue, Ardmore, Pennsylvania 19003, (215) 896-0860.

The fact that designers have the opportunity to work with talented type designers opens up the world of the past as well as the future. Picture this. You're browsing through your favorite bookstore and you find an old type specimen book of metal faces. You sigh wistfully. "Wasn't type beautiful then? The cut, the individuality of each face. Oh, this Electra would be perfect for the captions of the annual Christmas catalog. If only I could have it on my Mac...."

Do it!

36

Educating Your Clients

Congratulations! After a lot of hard work and long hours, you have transformed your design practice. You and your staff are computer-literate. You've completed a number of jobs in a shorter amount of time and at lower cost than you did with traditional tools. Your clients are delighted and are sending you more work *and* referrals.

Many of you provide design guidelines to corporations, publishing firms, universities, and the like that are responsible for their own production. You've probably taken the logical step of suggesting that you deliver the guidelines in electronic form (for example, on disk) so that they can carry out the production on their own computers. But what if they don't already own computers? Or, as often happens, the system they do have is a) inappropriate for their production tasks, b) incomplete, and/or c) something they don't know how to use?

As I said in chapter 22, "Keeping Up with Your Clients," part of your work requires advising your clients about the best methods of production, and therefore it's essential that you become knowledgeable about computer-based tools.

Now your clients are asking you for additional consultation. They're asking you to recommend what hardware and software configuration they should buy; what's more, they're asking you to teach them how to use it.

You may think that computer consultation strays too far outside the boundaries of graphic design. So should you simply say forget it?

No way. First, there are no rules that say where graphic design ends and another profession begins. Second, you must provide direction for your clients. You can't leave them with an unknown ending when you've given them such a promising beginning. The question is, to what extent will you be personally involved in delivering this direction?

Your actual involvement may be as little as a reference to a firm that you know provides the right computer consultation, or as much as taking on the entire job yourself. Or something in between, working in collaboration with a computer consulting firm.

One of the biggest benefits you get from advising your clients about buying and using computers is that you can ensure compatibility. If you've had any experience trying to share files with another hardware or software configuration, you know that the process can be exasperating. The marketplace is full of software programs and hardware peripherals that are similar in price and performance. By advising a client at the outset to purchase the same basic platform as yours, you can avoid many incompatibility problems.

This leads to another benefit. By getting your client to make an electronic commitment, you have helped to cement your relationship with that client. With this investment in setting up a smooth workflow, your client will have additional incentive to continue to send you work.

And, of course, it's additional income.

So all you have to do is give them a list of what you have, then tell them how you learned to use it.

Right?

Wrong.

Educating Your Clients

Sure, it would be easy to tell your clients exactly what you did (with adjustments based on your mistakes). But in all likelihood, their needs are not duplicates of yours. You have 5 people; they have 25. You work in three rooms; they work in three states. Your work is primarily design; theirs is production. You get the picture. The basic platform can be the same, but they may require different models of machines, more storage capacity, a more sophisticated network, different file management, and so forth. Having the knowledge to advise clients about these issues requires a serious investment of research time: You would have to study your clients' needs and keep abreast of the products that are appropriate. Some of that research will be relevant in your own studio, and some will serve only one client's unique problem. Do you have the resources to conduct this research? You must determine whether or not you want to have the expertise on your staff.

There's also a different emphasis on what your clients have to learn. While you may concentrate on the secrets of electronic lay-out, they may need to master a program's editing features. Your clients will also want a teaching program. If you learned by the seat of your pants, you know there's a better way for your clients. Again, do you have the resources to develop that plan and to carry it out? Or is it better to refer clients elsewhere?

I'm not advising one direction over another. I am advising you to be aware of the new needs of your clients, so that *you* can define the boundaries of your business and choose where to put your resources. One way or another, your clients need an answer. Whatever level of personal involvement you choose, you have an opportunity to gain a competitive edge by showing your clients that you can provide a solution.

The next time you present a comp at a client meeting and they ask you *how* you cropped a picture rather than *why,* be ready for the next question: What should we buy and how will we learn to use it?

♦ Update: See chapter 37, "Computers in the Studio," for a look at designers who have expanded their services for their clients.

37

....

Computers in the Studio

When I first walked into the office of Burns, Connacher & Waldron, I thought, "This is a classic design studio. White walls, big windows, good music." There was design paraphernalia stuck on the walls, large tables with pieces of Pantone spread around, and cans of spray mount. The Macintosh computers on every desk weren't out of place; they looked normal. But after being in the office for an hour, I found out: BCW is not a typical design studio.

►Left to right: Bob Burns, Martin Haggland, Jim Waldron, Michael Crumpton, Nat Connacher.

Micro*Color*

▶Martin scanned the logo for MicroColor and traced it in Illustrator. Then he used Studio/8 to give it a granite-fill pattern.

I got my first hint when something on one of the Mac screens caught my eye. It was an image that looked distinctly as if it had been etched in granite. But this was a computer screen! I said to the person sitting in front of the monitor, "How did you do that?" That immediately drew a crowd; the rest of the people in the office gathered around to see what I was looking at.

Martin Haggland, the owner of this screen, said, "Well, Nat [Connacher] designed my logo."

I interrupted him, "Your logo?"

"Yes, my company is MicroColor. I sublet space from BCW. And we work on some projects together." He continued with his explanation. "At the time Nat designed the logo, you couldn't get Univers 85 or Caslon swash caps, so we had the type set traditionally. Then I scanned the letters and traced them in [the program] Illustrator. One day, I decided to put my logo on my start-up screen. I copied the logo into [another program] Studio/8, and filled it with a 'granite-fill' pattern. I created highlights and dark areas to give it dimension. Then I copied that into PixelPaint, so that I could save it as a start-up screen."

Nat said, "Hey, we should design start-up screens for our clients." Then the group disbanded and went back to their own work. In a 30-second break, they learned a new technique and got a bright idea.

This is a typical scene at BCW. I was constantly aware of combinations: combinations of people, of materials, of expertise, and of software. Lots of software. In its first year and a half in business, Burns, Connacher & Waldron has become a design studio with a unique character emerging. Sometimes by design, sometimes by coincidence, sometimes even by mistake, it has created an atmosphere that is primed for the 1990s.

But this is not a success story about how wonderful computers are and how they saved money and lives. The studio developed in this way through nightmares and disasters, and having to come up with creative solutions.

Bob Burns, Nat Connacher, and Jim Waldron were graduate students at Yale, class of '87. By that time, computers were a given. Each student had a Macintosh and used it routinely for class assignments. Some used it more, some less.

So when the three of them laid the plans, on one snowy night at the Gypsy Bar in New Haven, to open a studio in the heart of the Big Apple (West 19th Street and Sixth Avenue), computers were barely mentioned. While the $20,000 worth of computers–including hardware and software and peripherals–that they budgeted was no small potatoes, there was never a doubt that computers would be part of the working environment. Nor was there a question about what kind to buy. They had been raised on the Macintosh, and Jim had worked at Apple for a summer. Each of them had experience working in the world of traditional tools, and at Yale they had learned about the advantages of using computers: the cost savings for themselves and for their clients.

One of the first jobs BCW landed was a corporate-identity program for a large financial firm in Toronto: Gordon Capital.

Using computers is a natural in the design and implementation of a corporate ID program, because the designer must give the client guidelines to follow. By giving these guidelines in electronic form, clients can carry out much of the production themselves. If they have in-house equipment, they can cut their typesetting and production expenses dramatically for in-house work, especially where a laser printer will suffice.

An integral part of BCW's work was to advise Gordon Capital

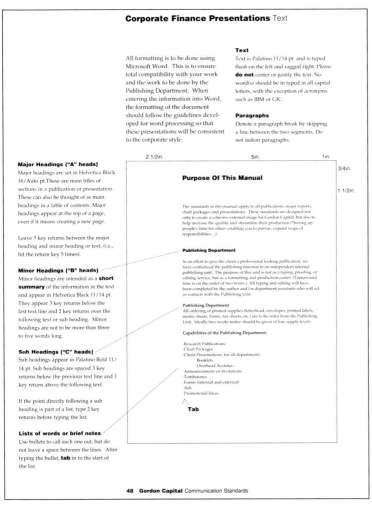

Corporate Finance Presentations Text

All formatting is to be done using Microsoft Word. This is to ensure total compatibility with your work and the work to be done by the Publishing Department. When entering the information into Word, the formatting of the document should follow the guidelines developed for word processing so that these presentations will be consistent to the corporate style.

Text

Text is Palatino 11/14 pt. and is typed flush on the left and ragged right. Please **do not** center or justify the text. No word(s) should be in typed in all capital letters, with the exception of acronyms such as IBM or GIC.

Paragraphs

Denote a paragraph break by skipping a line between the two segments. Do not indent paragraphs.

Major Headings ("A" heads)

Major headings are set in Helvetica Black 16/Auto pt. These are main titles of sections in a publication or presentation. These can also be thought of as main headings in a table of contents. Major headings appear at the top of a page, even if it means creating a new page.

Leave 5 key returns between the major heading and minor heading or text, (i.e., hit the return key 5 times).

Minor Headings ("B" heads)

Minor headings are intended as a **short summary** of the information in the text and appear in Helvetica Black 11/14 pt. They appear 3 key returns below the last text line and 2 key returns over the following text or sub heading. Minor headings are not to be more than three to five words long.

Sub Headings ("C" heads)

Sub headings appear in Palatino Bold 11/14 pt. Sub headings are spaced 3 key returns below the previous text line and 1 key return above the following text.

If the point directly following a sub heading is part of a list, type 2 key returns before typing the list.

Lists of words or brief notes

Use bullets to call each one out, but do not leave a space between the lines. After typing the bullet, **tab** in to the start of the list.

2 1/2in.   5in.   1in.

3/4in.

Purpose Of This Manual

1 1/2in.

The standards in this manual apply to all publications, major reports, chart packages and presentations. These standards are designed not only to create a cohesive external image for Gordon Capital, but also to help increase the quality and streamline their production ("freeing up people's time for other- enabling you to pursue, expand scope of responsibilities....).

Publishing Department

In an effort to give the client a professional looking publication, we have centralized the publishing function in an independent internal publishing unit. The purpose of this unit is not as a typing, proofing, or editing service, but as a formatting and production center. (Turnaround time is on the order of two hours.) All typing and editing will have been completed by the author and/or department assistants who will act as contacts with the Publishing Unit.

Publishing Department

All ordering of printed supplies (letterhead, envelopes, printed labels, memo sheets, forms, fax sheets, etc.) are to be order from the Publishing Unit. Ideally two weeks notice should be given of low supply levels.

Capabilities of the Publishing Department:

·Research Publications
·Chart Packages
·Client Presentations, for all departments
        Booklets
        Overhead Acetates
·Announcements or Invitations
·Tombstones
·Forms (internal and external)
·Ads
·Promotional Ideas

∧
Tab

▶BCW produced electronic and hard-copy guidelines for Gordon Capital's corporate ID program.

about computers for in-house production.

A major part of the proposal was an estimate of cost and time savings gained from bringing desktop publishing technology in-house. Typesetting for tombstones (the ads for stock in financial papers), for example, has gone from as high as $800 to as low as $20 per ad. Laser prints have replaced bluelines for signing off on typographic corrections.

BCW pushed hard to get Gordon Capital to use the same software and hardware configuration as BCW, so they could send, say, a form design via modem to Toronto, and Gordon could make modifications when necessary.

But having the same technology does not ensure smooth going.

Nat was ready for the big marketing meeting in Toronto. He planned to have a copy of the standards manual for each member of the meeting, and flew to Toronto the day before with 15 floppy disks. There were some last-minute changes the staff in Toronto wanted to make, and since Gordon Capital had the same hardware and software setup as the office of BCW, Nat figured the staff could make the changes at Gordon and print them out there.

The changes were made in Toronto, as planned. Then they tried to print. They clicked the simple command *print* and waited. And waited. Then they asked the most frightening question a designer can hear when using computers on a tight deadline: "What's wrong?" Nat prayed that it was some minor oversight. After several frantic phone calls and investigation, he discovered the worst. In major portions of the standards manual, he had used an early printer version of Helvetica. Way back in the old days of 1987, a font was *initialized* (essentially linked) to one laser printer. Most of the manual would print out only on his laser printer in his studio—yes, in New York. There was no way to print out on any other printer.

They typed the corrections on hard copy in Toronto and faxed them that night to the studio in New York. Jim and Bob were in the office until 1 A.M. making corrections and printing them out on the one and only laserwriter that could handle that particular job. At 8 A.M. Serena Koh, the office manager, took 20 copies of the standards by plane to Toronto; she arrived just in time for the 10:30 meeting.

It's not enough to have the same system configuration. You must also have the same *versions* of the system configuration. Even then there will be surprises. But surprises happen less and less as you gain more experience.

Experience. This is the big issue. BCW has learned that it must ask prospective employees, in the words of Jimi Hendrix, "But first, are you experienced?" It's easy for a novice who has learned by the seat of the pants to do things wrong. BCW warns of dangerous situations that can arise when a design firm hires temporary help. Mac Temps are the mechanical pasteup people of the future. But it is required to know much more than pasteup. How can you make sure people really know their stuff? "Give them a test drive!" says Jim.

And what about the roles? What skills should designers acquire, and what skills should they hire? You can't match the people to traditional roles. Typically, when you hire people full-time to do pasteup, there's a clear hierarchy, and they expect to get more and more design work. But when you hire someone for his or her software abilities, you're not hiring an apprentice. You're creating a team with complementary expertise–like a pilot and a navigator.

After BCW had been in business for about two months, it got a job that called for isometric drawings. Coincidentally, Michael Crumpton, an illustrator particularly adept at using sophisticated drawing software, had come by to show his book the day before. Jim called him, and Michael started working on the project right away.

Michael graduated from the Rhode Island School of Design, where he studied photography, illustration, and sculpture. He became interested in computers in 1987 and "looked over a friend's shoulder" for three months. He devoted all of his time to learning how to use drawing software programs.

When BCW's project was finished, Michael kept coming in to the office. Jim said, "Look, we don't always have work for you, but if you want to come in and use the computers, go ahead." Michael says, "Now I live here."

Jim's generosity was also shrewd. It was clear that Michael was good, and was constantly learning more. BCW wanted to keep the relationship, but of course didn't want to have to pay for the learning time. It wanted the benefits of learning what the programs could do, and it wanted to have an accessible free-lance illustrator. So BCW offered to let Michael use equipment (Michael had none, and needed a lot) and offered him a low rent. It was great for Michael: He needed equipment, but even more than that, he needed real problems to solve.

He got problems. Each job is a lesson in the discrepancies among the computer's screen, the laser printer, and high-resolution type-set output. Because of the vastly different resolution (from 72 to 2,400 dots per inch), the type, line art, tint screens, and rules look quite different from one medium to the next. Michael learned the golden rule: Test, test, test. They printed out and typeset variations on screen tints, type, and so on. Jim said, "We had good intentions about creating internal manuals showing these variations, but we never had the time. Besides, we're all in constant touch with each other, so it's not necessary." Also, since they were creating separate overlays on film for the printer, they had to worry about trapping. "When we did the separate overlays, we were very lucky. We found out later that if you run film out at different times, you can get different densities. With a different temperature, the film might expand, and all your traps will be off."

As the programs become more sophisticated, there is much more to learn. Graphic design is a complex set of tasks. It's no surprise that the new tools that help you to do all those tasks are also complex. And as more products come out, you must understand how they affect each other.

The more you push a program, the more you bump up against its limitations. Fortunately, the software vendor usually comes out with upgrades that address those limitations. As you learn more, you want to do more. So you're eager to keep up with the latest features. As Jim says, "If you went to sleep for six months, then woke up and kept using the old programs, you'd be so out of it."

It's a seductive loop. The more you invest, the more you can save. But it's impossible to maintain a consistent, stable level. As you become aware of the new technology available, you realize that you could reap even greater benefits by taking advantage of it. But in order to do so, you must once again invest in the time and mistakes it takes to learn. It's the ominous J curve: You become less productive before you become more productive.

That requires a balancing act. BCW has a natural rhythm for keeping the learning consistent with the doing, so the learning time pays off. Once the designers know a program's capabilities, they know which jobs will go smoothly. Bob had a job to design a project for a Yale University fellowship program, which included stationery, an invitation, and so on. There was an existing logo, but it needed to be refined. And the client didn't have any artwork, so it had to be redrawn. Michael used Aldus FreeHand to redraw the Hebrew characters and to place the type—Palatino—in a circle. He finished the seal in about two

►Michael used Aldus FreeHand to redraw the Hebrew characters and place the type in a circle.

►This logo was created in Aldus FreeHand.

hours, and BCW now has artwork that can be electronically re-sized to any dimensions. The logo for the Zoological Society was also created in Aldus FreeHand. Michael used Adobe Illustrator for a set of complex building drawings.

BCW wants to capitalize on its knowledge of the computer. The designers don't want to just use the technology; they want to sell their expertise. As a result of their networking—going to trade shows, frequenting service bureaus and visiting colleagues who work in the computer industry—BCW has sought and landed jobs that could be labeled "design research."

BCW, MicroColor, and Michael are all working together on a huge project. Unfortunately, they can't tell me what the project is, or who it's for, because it's confidential. They could tell me this much: Because BCW has experience both in design and in exploring

Design and Technology

▶Michael used Adobe Illustrator to draw this complex set of buildings.

the capabilities of computers, they have been contracted to experiment with a vendor's new line of hardware and software in the area of color for desktop publishing. They subcontracted to Micro-Color because of Martin's expertise in traditional and computer-related color separation. In this job, they have crossed a line–now they are selling a service to the computer industry–and, because of the exploratory nature of their work, they are becoming a part of the industry.

When we left the studio for dinner, Bob turned the music up loud, Jim turned the alarm system on, and I lost count of how many locks Nat locked. I said, "I know we're in New York, but isn't this a bit elaborate?" On the way to the restaurant, they told me about the break-ins. "First they stole a MacPlus and a hard disk. Then they came back a week later and took an SE and two hard disks and a carrying case." I thought it was all pretty scary, and mumbled something about erasing such an awful thing from your memory. Thinking I was referring to losing what had been stored on their hard disks, Jim said, "No, it's OK. We were insured for data loss."

Out of the eighties, into the nineties.

CASE 1: ANNUAL REPORT

This is the first of three anecdotes. They're BCW's all-too-real stories of the pros and cons of a design studio using computers:

The Dataflex annual report was BCW's third job. The company was intent on producing a good job at a low cost. It was only a 20-page book. It looked so doable.

At the time, a colleague with a lot of experience in annual report design was working at BCW. But she didn't have a lot of experience with the Macintosh. She learned as she designed. Jim said, "We told her to just go ahead and to ask us if she had any questions." She learned on her own, with others around to help her out when she got stuck. Because she was learning a new technology, this design took her about four times as long as she'd normally take. Because they're conversant with page layout programs, Jim, Bob, and Nat generally use the Mac in their design stage because they can work much faster with it than they do with traditional tools.

The design comps for the annual report were created using a combination of Aldus PageMaker and LaserWriter output, INTs, and stock photography. The comps were accepted with minor revisions.

Serena Koh, the office manager at BCW, input (typed, as they said in the old days) the text from faxed copy. Serena and Jim both proofed the input copy. "We realized later that we should have hired a typist and proofreader," said Jim.

When his colleague's contract with BCW ended, Jim took on the production. The 20 pages of the annual report were stored in the computer, essentially ready to be typeset as fully laid-out pages, with everything camera-ready except the photos. All that was left to do was plug in the real numbers (as usual with an annual report, the financial data were not ready) and the corrections to the text. Jim opened the file and brought the first spread to the screen. He got a sinking feeling—the first of many—as he waited for all the elements of the pages to appear on the screen. "Why is this taking so long?" And then, "Why is it taking eons to print this out?" He began investigating, and finally found his colleague's mistake.

Learning on her own, she had not fully understood the way "cut" and "paste" works on the computer. She had inadvertently made some of the type white, and had "pasted" a block of type on top of itself, often as many as three times, on many different blocks of text. Somehow she had made the top layer black, so it showed up. Her mistakes weren't evident on the printouts.

It wasn't until Jim took over her work that he realized that there was a problem. Once he figured it out, he erased the superfluous text blocks. As in any project, a document acquires a history of all who have worked on it. But the problem is compounded with a computer because much of the work is intangible. Placing an element on a page is an act of faith; you can't touch it.

Jim made the corrections and plugged in the real numbers. All that was left to do was send the disk to the service bureau for repro.

Computers in the Studio

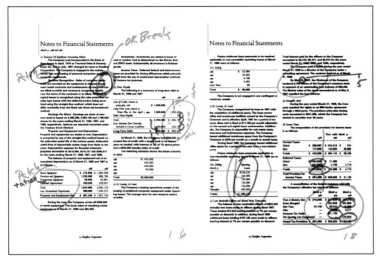

▶The first set of changes from the client is marked with author's alterations and printer's errors.

Whoa, not so fast. The first set of changes from the client came in, marked with author's alterations and printer's errors. Lots of them. "From that point on," Jim said, "I was completely a typesetter."

Add a line of type here, take away a line there. The beauty of electronic page layout made the changes a breeze; he typed in characters, and the text automatically reflowed, maintaining all of its specifications. The additions created extra lines of text; the last lines moved beyond the allowed text grid. Jim removed the extra lines, but in his rush he forgot to add them on the next page. He didn't catch the plus sign, PageMaker's indicator that extra text needs to be placed.

When the client received the proof, he said, "Where's the last line? It was here last time!" Jim knew the problem immediately. It's the electronic equivalent of losing a piece of repro and finding it later on your sock.

Then came the next revision. There were misspellings. All the numbers were new, which caused the pages to change dramatically. Nothing lined up. "We manually hyphenated or broke lines to make it look good." This is a definite no-no. If you manually insert a line break, and changes are made later, you'll still have a line break at that word. Jim's lack of experience in the finer points of typesetting was compounded by the clients' lack of experience with annual reports; this was only their second.

After six revisions, the proofs were all approved. Jim sent the job out for Linotronic output–rush, of course. The nice thing about a rush job with electronic layout is that rush–double charge–is only $20 a page. When Jim got the repro back, he looked at the first page and was horrified.

He had never run the pages off in repro. The comps and all the proofs were output on the laser printer, and he had been judging the typeface weights according to the proofs. The actual repro made it painfully obvious that the type for the heads was too light and didn't stand out enough against the bold. So Jim boosted the heads up one point size. That was easy to do; he had saved all the specs for the heads in a "style sheet." By changing the style sheet, the heads changed automatically. He had the job typeset again (rush, again) and developed the umpteenth ulcer while waiting. He got the repro back and pasted up the entire job in an hour.

"You know," Jim said, "those are full pages with crop marks, and that was the fastest 20-page pasteup ever."

The boards were ready to go. The client decided that he wanted to hang the brackets. Jim swore, after two sets of typeset output, he wouldn't take the job off the boards again. It's cumbersome to create hanging brackets in a page layout program, and Jim thought the revisions were over, so he cut and pasted by hand, I mean *really* by hand, 35 brackets.

Then there were more AAs. By now Jim had to set and patch by hand, because he had made manual changes and the electronic version was no longer up-to-date. At that point, electronic production came to a halt.

The final piece looked good, but BCW had to eat the mistakes.

After Jim told me this story, we discussed the vast amount of knowledge he'd gained since learning new features of the programs and hiring the right kind of help. I asked Jim if he would ever take on another annual report. He thought for a moment, then said, "Yes. Because I know more now."

CASE 2: POSTERS

Vincent Gleason, head of publications at the National Park Service in Washington, D.C., urgently needed posters for public awareness of drug abuse in the parks. He requested that Bob Burns come to a Thursday meeting. Gleason wanted color comps of four posters by the following Tuesday.

There was no copy, only the general concept. Bob had four days to develop the concept, copy, and design and to produce the comps. And it happened to be over a weekend, difficult for services. On top of that, both of Bob's partners were out of town.

On the shuttle home, Bob developed his ideas. He decided to use flat color shapes. Because of the short deadline, photography was out of the question.

Bob was familiar with drawing programs and knew he could create his sketches and comps using a mixture of software and traditional tools. He asked illustrator Michael Crumpton to create some pills, leaves, a boot, a hand.

▶Sketches and laser printout.

Michael printed out the elements, and Bob developed the formal arrangements on tissue. Then they worked together at the computer. Using a combination of an Adobe Illustrator (a drawing program) and Quark XPress (a page layout program), they worked out the text, typography, shapes, and formal composition for each poster by Sunday afternoon.

Bob often used the Mac for black-and-white comps, but when

▶Color
thermal
transfer
printout.

it came to color, no color output satisfied him. For the poster series, Bob assumed he would be cutting Pantone paper and having INTs made for the final comps. He budgeted Monday for production.

Jim got back Sunday night and stopped at the office. As soon as he saw what Bob was doing, he said, "You should use the QMS (ColorScript) printer. It would be perfect for making the comps." Bob was skeptical about the quality, but after some convincing by Jim and after looking at samples, he said OK.

He also went out and bought all the Pantone paper he needed—just in case. "I gave myself a deadline of 3 P.M. Monday. If the technology failed, I still had all afternoon and night to do the production."

Bob called the service bureau first thing Monday morning and reserved time on the Mac II. You need a Mac to send files to the color printer.

Bob and Michael spent the entire day and evening at the service bureau. First they had to deal with color deviations. The color on the monitor is different from the color on the printout, which is different from Pantone color. They had to make a number of printouts to get the colors they wanted.

▶Computer
screens show
close-ups of
color
selections.

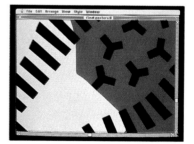

Suddenly the printer didn't show up on the network. No one knew what to do. Michael suggested turning the machine on and off, twice, a piece of magic he'd often had success with. It worked.

Then the printer started substituting Courier for Helvetica. After a while they figured out that some other customer must have replaced Bob's fonts. Another network problem.

Bob was on edge all morning, ready to go for the Pantone paper. By early afternoon, things were going smoothly. They were getting good colors, excellent comps. They printed out variations on 8½ x 11 sheets, making choices based on the best color combinations. They planned to print the final comps on 11 x 17.

It was past Bob's deadline when they discovered the service bureau had run out of tabloid-size paper. Small comps would have to do.

On Tuesday, August 16, Bob flew to Washington and presented the comps. They were approved. On Wednesday, Gleason called. "We need to change the word *disease* to *cancer,* and we need to see a mountain range in one of the backgrounds. And we need the comps by Friday."

Bob made the changes and brought the disks to the service bureau. He made four new comps in less than an hour.

On Tuesday, August 23, Gleason requested an extra set of comps with a few minor text changes by Thursday and mechanicals by Friday.

Instead of feeling sick every time his client asked for changes, Bob felt fine. He felt even better when he did the mechanicals. Instead of spending three days inking all those drawings, he simply sent his disks to a service bureau to be set on a Linotronic at high resolution.

This was the first time Bob used computers for the entire process, from concept to production. "The savings," he said, "made me a true believer."

▶Four printed posters, created with computers from start to finish.

Computers in the Studio

COMPREHENSIVE PRODUCTION: 4 COMPS

TRADITIONAL MATERIALS		ELECTRONIC MATERIALS	
24 sheets Pantone @ $7 each	$168	Mac II rental	
Typesetting rush	$250	12 hours @ $40/hour	$480
INTs	$350	36 color printouts @ $10 each	$360
Deliveries	$ 40		
Total	$808	Total	$840
Traditional time	12 hrs	Electronic time	34 hrs

FIRST REVISION: 4 COMPS

TRADITIONAL MATERIALS		ELECTRONIC MATERIALS	
12 sheets Pantone @ $7 each	$ 84	Mac II rental 1 hour	$ 40
Typesetting rush	$250	4 color printouts @ $14 each	$ 56
INTs	$350		
Deliveries	$ 40		
Total	$724	Total	$ 96
Traditional time	12 hrs	Electronic time	1 hr

► This table shows the savings in time and costs by creating the posters entirely by computer.

SECOND REVISION: 4 COMPS

TRADITIONAL MATERIALS		ELECTRONIC MATERIALS	
12 sheets Pantone @ $7 each	$ 84	Mac II rental 1 hour	$ 40
Typesetting rush	$250	4 color printouts @ $14 each	$ 56
INTs	$350		
Deliveries	$ 40		
Total	$724	Total	$ 96
Traditional time	12 hrs	Electronic time	.5 hrs

MECHANICALS

TRADITIONAL TIME		ELECTRONIC TIME	
All drawings to be inked	21 hrs	Drawings already complete	
Type was already set		Type was already set	
Pasteup	4 hrs	Pasteup	4 hrs

GRAND TOTALS

Traditional materials	$2,256	Electronic materials	$1,032
Traditional time	61 hrs	Electronic time	39.5 hrs

CASE 3: HYPERCARD STACK

BCW has completed several design projects in which the final viewing medium is not print but the computer itself. One of the products it has used is a program called HyperCard. HyperCard is, among other things, a system for storing and retrieving sound, text, and graphics on a computer. You can customize this information to create a visual data base. Jim Waldron is one of the HyperCard cognoscenti.

"When I saw the introduction for HyperCard," Jim said, "my reaction was, big deal. People were using it for making electronic indexing. Then, about a year later, I saw a HyperCard project that a medical illustrator did. He illustrated and animated heart ailments, and he had easy-to-understand diagrams. I got very excited because it was well designed and I learned something. I thought I'd like to design in that medium, but I didn't have a client for it. So, for the next few weeks, I learned on the weekends, trying to put together a demo so I could sell the idea to a client.

"We were making a history of the Brooklyn Bridge when suddenly a real problem was given to us. We were doing print work for a client, Agfa Compugraphic, and they were about to announce some products for the Macintosh environment. I realized that a Hyper-Card stack would be perfect for them to show at MacWorld. So I did a demo, and when they saw it, they bought the idea. Soon after, we had another opportunity to create a stack for Kensington, and we already had a demo to show. Now we have a portfolio of 'hypermedia.' Because of that initial spec work, we're doing a number of very profitable jobs."

►BCW developed a HyperCard demonstration showing Agfa Compugraphic's typefaces and products.

Computers in the Studio

Turbo Mouse Top Ten

Click on any of the topics below for more information.

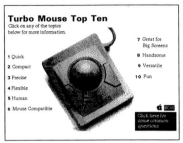

7 Great for Big Screens

8 Handsome

9 Versatile

10 Fun

1 Quick

2 Compact

3 Precise

4 Flexible

5 Human

6 Mouse Compatible

Click here for some common questions

■ Compact

No rolling room required.

With the Turbo Mouse ball on top, you move only the ball, not the whole mouse.

Back to Top Ten

■ Precise

Turbo Mouse is twice as precise as a mouse.

New patented "optical levering" technology offers 200 CPI pin-point precision.

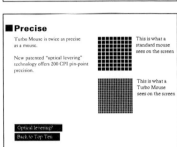

This is what a standard mouse sees on the screen

This is what a Turbo Mouse sees on the screen

Optical levering?

Back to Top Ten

■ Human

Advanced two-button design allows for either right or left-handed use!

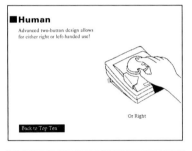

Or Right

Back to Top Ten

►Printout of HyperCard stack for Kensington.

■ Great for Big Screens

For big screen users, there's Turbo Mouse Custom Control Panel software for even greater speed and flexibility.

The Turbo Mouse Custom Control Panel offers a "Very Fast" Tracking Speed not found in the standard Mouse settings. And it lets you customize your Turbo Mouse settings to select cursor and double-click speeds in between the standard mouse settings.

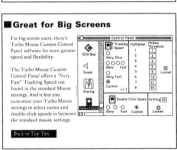

Back to Top Ten

■ Mouse Compatible

Turbo Mouse let you continue to use your old mouse if you want to.

Turbo Mouse Plus offers a second mouse port. Turbo Mouse ADB offers a second ADB port.

Just plug your mouse into the Turbo Mouse and you can switch back and forth instantly between the two.

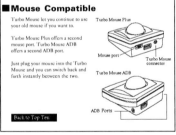

Turbo Mouse Plus

Mouse port

Turbo Mouse connector

Turbo Mouse ADB

ADB Ports

Back to Top Ten

■ Versatile

Turbo Mouse comes in two models, compatible with any Macintosh.

Turbo Mouse ADB, model 62360, works with the Mac SE, Mac II, and Apple IIGS.

Turbo Mouse Plus, model 62358, works with Mac and Mac Plus.

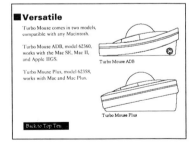

Turbo Mouse ADB

Turbo Mouse Plus

Back to Top Ten

■ Fun

Turbo Mouse is quicker, more versatile and much more fun than a traditional mouse.

Buy one today and you'll be putting your old mouse on the next flight to Florida.

Back to Top Ten

Design and Technology

BCW and MicroColor Hardware and Software List

Apple MacPlus (2)	Adobe Fonts
Jasmine Hard Disk (2)	Adobe Illustrator 88
Apple LaserWriter Plus	Agfa Compugraphic Fonts
Microtek Scanner	Aldus FreeHand
Apple Mac SE/30	Aldus PageMaker
Apple Mac II	Apple HyperCard Tools
Apple Color Monitor	AppleLink Software
Apple 40 MB Drive + 5 MB RAM	Avalon Development Group PhotoMac
Farralon MacRecorder	BPI Accounting
Apple Personal Modem	Caere OmniPage
US Robotics 9600 Baud Modem	Electronic Arts Studio/8
Apple MacIIx	Enabling Technologies Pro3D
Apple Color Monitor	LaserWare LaserPaint
Apple Hard Disk	Letraset ImageStudio
	MacroMind VideoWorks II
	Microsoft Excel
	Microsoft Word
	Microtek GreyScan II
	Microtek VersaScan
	Neoscribe International Fonts
	QuarkXPress
	Satori Project Billing
	Silicon Beach Digital Darkroom
	SuperMac PixelPaint
	Symantec Utilities

38

········

The Bottom Line

─────

Are you trying to decide whether or not to buy computers? If you've added up the costs, you know that you're going to have to justify these expensive items—to yourself, to your business partner, or to your boss. You have to think about the bottom line.

I called two colleagues—Tom Lewis of Tom Lewis, Inc., in Del Mar, California, and Will Sherwood of Will Sherwood Advertising Inc. in Panorama City, California—who have years of experience dealing with computers. They've looked at the numbers. I asked them if they would bare their financial souls, and am grateful for their candor. In the words of Socrates, "He who reflects on other men's insight will come easily by what they labored hard for."

TOM LEWIS, INC.

Tom bought his first computer (a Macintosh SE) in May 1987. As of May 1989, Tom Lewis, Inc., has five Macs and lots of peripherals, totaling about $33,000 worth of equipment and software.

"As an owner and manager of a graphic design firm," says Tom, "I'm concerned not only about our market position and staying current with design trends, ... but also ... I know that our success or ability to survive depends on the bottom line.

"While I was in the process of changing our traditional manner of work to electronic, questions came up: Is it cost-efficient? Does it pay for itself? Does it make financial sense? So I roughed up this evaluation. It was generated by a gut feeling. I began to find support in more specific information."

In 1985, its pre-Mac days, Tom Lewis, Inc., had a revenue of $680,000 and spent $47,000 for type. In May 1989 Tom looked at the amount it spent on type for roughly the same revenue ($600,000) and found that it had spent $14,000. For the same revenue, it paid $33,000 less for type ($47,000 minus $14,000). In the pre-Mac days, it charged the typical 15-20 percent markup for type. With the Mac, it charged the same as pre-Mac for the type. So, in addition to a profit of $33,000, it also has its 15-20 percent markup.

Tom looked at the cost of all his equipment at the time of this analysis. Coincidentally, the cost of the equipment was approximately $33,000! In other words, Tom said, "Where did the money come from to pay for this equipment? From the type!"

There's the cost of the equipment, sure. But there's also another cost: time.

I asked Tom, "How much time was lost in training?"

Tom answered, "It was time-intensive, slower when we first got equipment. Sometimes it was all really questionable. Day to day it was a real pain getting people squared away. Nonbillable time, downtime, was at an all-time high, in excess of 30-40 percent, so I figured that meant too many people. So people went away in 1987, and again in 1988. After the fact, I went back and looked at when we got the Macs. In looking back, I realize that as we put a Mac in, an employee went away. We got a Mac in May 1987, and removed a person in September 1987. We did *not* do this on purpose; I didn't think of it as replacing people with computers.

"When I did the analysis, I took the revenue from 1985 and divided by seven employees to see my revenue per employee. In round numbers, we went from $100,000 per employee in 1985 to $200,000 per employee in 1989."

I asked, "Did you drop or increase your rates?"

Tom said, "Neither. That concerns me the most. The way we set rates is from past experience. We have time cards so that we can evaluate what the *next* job will cost. Now the jobs take less time, but it would be wrong to reduce the cost because of the fact that we're more efficient! So how do we go about it? I don't know. The competition will probably get stiffer; the technology is giving us a lead now, but we may lose it. . . . There are a lot of unanswered questions.

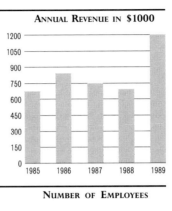

ANNUAL REVENUE IN $1000

NUMBER OF EMPLOYEES

NUMBER OF COMPUTERS

►Through several years of experience, Tom Lewis, Inc., developed a successful balance of employees, computers, and revenue.

"We had not thought of nonbillable time as an investment. Now we realize it was training. We haven't looked at the savings of having fewer employees. That's tremendous. Other numbers pale in comparison."

Now he is increasing the number of jobs, hiring people, and by the end of 1989 will have almost the same number of employees that he had in early 1987–and almost double the revenue.

WILL SHERWOOD ADVERTISING INC.

Will Sherwood of Sherwood Advertising Inc. decided early in 1986 to invest in a MacPlus, a LaserWriter, and page layout software. The company's original outlay was about $10,000. In February 1988 it bought a Lightspeed Color Layout System. It now has a range of equipment and software, worth about $75,000. It bought some of the equipment outright and is leasing the rest.

For example, Will decided to lease the Lightspeed system, which cost $44,730. He has a 60-month lease, and he pays $1,076 per month. Will has gone through the numbers, and has figured out that if he divides up the cost of equipment per employee, he ends up with $625 per month per person for the computer-related tools. That's a lot of overhead for an employee who already costs, say, $2,500 per month.

But wait. Will's people have kept track of their time and have found that they are much more productive using computers. Each one is, on average, as effective as 1.75 designers!

With computers, one designer costs $2,500 plus $625, or $3,125 per month. Without computers, Will would need 1.75 designers for every one designer to do the same amount of work. That would cost him, in salary, $4,375, as opposed to $3,125. Looking at it that way, he's saving $1,250 per month.

Of course there are many more factors, such as, again, training time. Will said that even though his people were productive within the first few days of using a program, they felt they needed about four weeks to be fluid, eight weeks to be a power user.

So let's say his people were on the down slope of the J curve for about two months, learning two software programs. He lost about two months of billable time per person. But as a result, after the two months they became 1.75 people each.

I asked Will about billing rates. He had this analysis: After eight weeks, the computer increases efficiency by 75 percent. So you can either increase hourly rates by 75 percent or reduce rates by 42.8 percent, as competitive situations allow.

Will called yesterday to add an interesting story.

"The First Los Angeles Bank wanted my company to do their annual report, but they had a quote from another firm for $29,000. No photos, simple charts. They said to me, 'If you can come in for under that price, you can have the job.' So I came in at $28,500.

Our costs for the job turned out to be $18,000 for everything— time, materials, everything. So we pocketed about $10,500."

39

Multimedia

In the past few chapters, I've talked about the time and money you have to invest before your computers really pay off. There's a lot to learn, and the equipment's not cheap. But once you've gotten a handle on the software, you can be much more productive, and you can get really creative.

Clement Mok of Clement Mok Design in San Francisco has a client that's a financial software management company. The name of the company, Pillar, presented good possibilities for the logo design, and suggested nice imagery. How should the imagery be used? Literally? Or should the imagery be abstract and read Pillar but suggest other things as well? When he presented his design of the company's logo, he wanted his client to understand its development.

Clement decided to make the presentation in a completely new way, and show the association of images. He created a simple Hyper-Card stack of images that dissolved from one picture to the next.

One of HyperCard's best and most effective uses is in presentation. It's a simple way to create and present a "slide show" on a computer monitor. With a couple of commands (such as "Go to

▶Selected frames from Clement's Pillar logo stack.

next card"), you can create an animation that runs automatically at the pace you specify, or you can advance to each frame, or card as they're called in HyperCard, by clicking the mouse.

Clement scanned a series of old engravings of banks and institutions with columns, and placed each image on a separate card to portray an association of pillars to banks. By dissolve, he superimposed a Bodoni *I* over a column. He explained his reasoning for his logo development as the animation progressed through 20 cards. The client loved it, because he literally saw the associations.

"It's harder to use words to describe an idea than it is to use visuals," Clement says. "Animation makes it easier to show how certain images evoke a word."

He used an animated sequence to show another client, an electronic mail company called Connect, how he developed the drawing of its logo. First he scanned in an image of a telephone cord, and showed the similarity of the shapes to the letter *N*. He played with bold and light letterforms and made a 10-card dissolve, showing the creation of the word *connect* from the cord.

Many of Clement's clients are software companies, and it's not unusual for them to request a "soft" brochure as well as a hard one. One company decided to use his animation of its logo to run

►Selected
frames from
Clement's
CONNECT logo
stack.

on the computer as part of its software package's guided tour.

Clement spent about 25 minutes creating these animations. They required no more hardware or software than he already owned, and no more learning. It just took imagination.

MTV Europe, the pan-European video and music channel, has commissioned a wide range of art students and professional animators to design MTV spots. Two professional design firms, Imagine and 4i Collaboration, designed and produced the title sequence on the "Braun European Top Twenty" show. (The show is produced by MTV and sponsored by Braun.) Using primarily typography, they created their frames with the software program Aldus FreeHand to stretch and wrap type, to align the type to a curve, and to create a lot of other typographic manipulations. Imagine's work is about 25 percent animation, 75 percent print, so the firm is familiar with the production requirements of both print and video, and what computer tools are available for both.

The team that worked on the animation has spent time in the editing suite as well as on the computer using FreeHand, and its members understand the best capabilities of each. Alan Sekers, the CEO of Imagine, describes the teams that work on these projects as "mutually dependent ecologies."

Each of the above design firms considers graphic design a multimedia discipline and is using computers to help realize the opportunities that exist in other media. This is just the beginning of a radical change that's in the air. Desktop media is something I consider much more significant to the design profession than desktop publishing.

Think about incorporating other media in *your* studio. You've put in a lot of effort to learn how to use computers, and it's finally paying off. Well, you've learned more than you may realize. Your knowledge of computers will aid in your education in other media.

The language of different professions is beginning to look more similar, a kind of Esperanto. I had an experience recently that made me realize that the computer is introducing a common language to different professions: the language of cut and paste.

I was working in an editing room at a video production facility recently, and Bill, one of the video editors, rolled a cart with a Mac II and a color monitor into an empty conference room.

He said, "Have you seen the program MacroMind Director? I tried it last night. Let me show you what it does."

I hadn't seen it, but I knew that Director was an animation program, a new and much more sophisticated version of Macro-Mind's earlier program, VideoWorks II.

Bill had created a simple cartoon of a guy in a flying saucer, and he made the saucer fly slowly across the screen. He opened a smaller window on the screen, the *score window.*

The score represents the cast members in the script and their frame numbers. In this case, a row of boxes was filled in that represented the guy in the saucer. Bill selected the row of frames, just as you would select a line of type in a page layout program. Then he cut the row and pasted it to a later place in the score. When he selected *play,* instead of appearing right away as the saucer had before, it appeared a few seconds later. It was exactly like cutting a paragraph of text and pasting it in a few pages later.

If you use a page layout program, then you can understand this, because the idea and the interaction is similar. You "import" pictures, three-dimensional drawings, or illustrations that you've scanned or manipulated in other programs, and you place them on the page, or in this case your stage. But now you have the additional dimension of time to work with.

Most graphic designers have resisted animation, video, and sound as part of their work. That's understandable. The services and tools of those disciplines are intimidating and costly. But that's changing.

The computer is the pivotal element that will make professions overlap to create new teams and new projects. Presentations that used to be restricted to one medium will combine print, still images, sound, and video because all of these elements can be displayed or output from one workstation.

Most of us who have a computer insisted on buying the best we could afford. Often the best meant which would have the longest life before it became obsolete. A computer that would remain useful in the future is one that can be expanded, that is, one to which you can add pieces.

It's likely that your computer is capable of much more than you're using it for. If you have a Mac II, and you open it up, you'll probably see a lot of empty space inside. Computer companies have been busy making the products that will expand your computer's capabilities. You can add a video board that gives your monitor millions of colors instead of thousands. You can add video digitizers to capture an image from a video camera or a VCR. You can attach a CD-ROM drive so that you can buy CD-ROMs that store thousands of stock photographs or clip art drawings to use in your work. You can add a graphics overlay board and display full-motion video on your computer's monitor, with an overlay of type and graphics.

By the way, multimedia is by no means limited to Apple computers. Amiga, the computer from Commodore, has been a favorite in the video world since long before Apple even had color. The National Association of Broadcasters gave Amiga the award of Most Useful Video Product of 1988. It has a 29 percent market share of character generators. Animators love the machine, but graphic designers have barely touched it, even though it's cheaper than a Mac. The main problem with Amiga is a lack of software, especially in print-related products. It may develop a stronger showing in multimedia. Other companies are eyeing the market as well. At a recent multimedia trade show in San Francisco, IBM had the largest booth.

The computer is making it easier for graphic designers to embrace other media as part of the profession. Now you produce comps for print pieces. Why not consider producing animated storyboards for a cable TV station identification?

New tools give you access to disciplines that you could never touch before. The possibilities leave desktop publishing in the dust. Desktop publishing tools are replacement tools. Multimedia tools are new tools, and they bring you into completely new areas of visual communication.

40

....

Interactive Media

In the previous chapter I talked about how the tools of different design professions are merging into one workstation: the multimedia workstation.

Now let's go a step further. The same workstation you use as a tool to create mechanicals or animations is also a setup on which to view final results. When you add a videodisc player, a television monitor, a large data base of visual information, plus a well-designed interface, then you have an information station.

Information is the product of the 1990s. (Just ask Richard Saul Wurman.) There's a move afoot to give the consumer, business-person, and student new ways of accessing and digesting information. The buzz term is *interactive media*.

In 1987 WGBH Educational Foundation (Channel 2, Boston's public television station) approached Apple Computer, Inc., with a new idea. It wanted to develop an interactive learning program for secondary school students using one of its "NOVA" science shows as the basis. WGBH is a major producer of PBS shows, and "NOVA" is perhaps its best known. An Interactive NOVA program would let the student control the speed, sequence, and depth of his or her

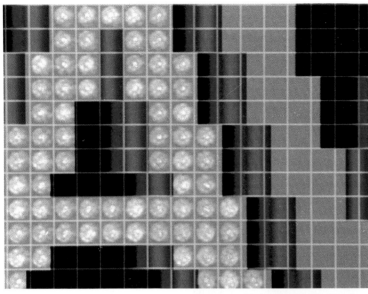

►In 1981, Paul Souza designed the opening sequence for "NOVA." He worked with computer programmers at the New York Institute of Technology to create animations of a "cosmic zoom" of scientific imagery.

learning. The student would investigate a "multimedia data base."

The episode that WGBH chose was "The Mystery of Animal Pathfinders," a 1986 "NOVA" show produced by Peace River Films. The film footage would be expanded upon; there would be supporting photography, video, graphics, and textual information, collected and/or commissioned. A graphic structure would be created to give the student a clear and enticing way to learn and explore.

What a project for a designer! Enter Paul Souza.

►To produce the NOVA book, Paul worked with Scitex operators to make the color separations.

Paul Souza has been a designer at WGBH since 1977, and has taken advantage of just about every piece of technology he could get his hands on. The results have won him many design awards.

Design and Technology

The list of computers he's battled with should be painted as little icons on the side of his car: Scitex, Lightspeed, Quantel Paintbox, Aurora 125, 220, 280, Amiga, IBM PC, Apple IIGS and of course the Macintosh. As one of Paul's colleagues said, "There are defensive learners and aggressive learners. Paul is an aggressive learner."

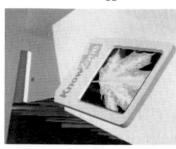

▶In 1986, Paul designed the opening scene for "KnowZone," a WGBH children's program. He used the Macintosh and software programs EZ3D and VideoWorks to plan the animation.

▶Cover and spread from WGBH's proposal for Interactive NOVA.

For the past three years, Paul has been the designer for Interactive NOVA, and the project has taken advantage of his unique combination of talents and knowledge in print, video, animation, and computers.

Paul's challenge began with the proposal. WGBH proposals were typically produced on a typewriter and copier, because only a few copies were needed. Paul decided to do the proposal on the Mac and LaserWriter. Using the Mac Plus and PageMaker 1.1, Paul produced what turned out to be a massive proposal–298 pages–an incredible amount of work with PageMaker 1.1. (His work earned Aldus's first prize of a trip to Italy.) The proposal was accepted. WGBH worked with Peace River Films and Apple Computer, Inc., to expand the "NOVA" program into Interactive NOVA.

The Interactive NOVA setup is a standard Mac Plus, SE, or Mac II, with a hard disk. The computer screen serves two functions: It's the "control panel" with buttons that let the student select other cards or film clips or photographs on the videodiscs; the computer screen also displays textual and graphical information, stills, and animation.

The full-motion video and full-color imagery are stored on two videodiscs, which play on a videodisc player with a color video monitor.

A videodisc holds 54,000 frames of still images and/or video sequences on each side. Still images speed by at the rate of 30 per second! Alternatively, each side of the disc can hold a half hour of full-motion video. Add a computer to control the videodisc, and you have random access, like an audio CD. By clicking on a selection on the computer screen, you can go to any image on the disc immediately, without having to rewind or fast-forward.

Interactive NOVA consists of four major areas:

The Overview includes video sequences that give an overall explanation, plus the original hour-long show.

The Data Base, which is the richest portion, includes hundreds—perhaps thousands—of "pages" or cards in HyperCard. The cards, which appear on the Macintosh screen, have textual information and the control buttons that let you access any video frame or sequence from the videodiscs. Those video images appear on the TV monitor.

The Activities are video sequences, animation, and games that encourage the viewer to make selections to solve mysteries about animal migration.

The Resources are reference materials and a "Report Maker." Students can use the tools in Report Maker to create their own sequence of stills and videos, and to write their own text.

Designing for an interactive videodisc project presents a very different set of design problems than a noninteractive project, such as a book. A reader always knows where he or she is in a book—beginning, middle, or end. A book is meant to be read linearly. Interactive media is meant to be viewed in any order the viewer wants. Viewers need visual clues to know where they are, and how to get to where they want to go.

▶The basic setup for Interactive NOVA: On the left is a Mac Plus with a hard disk. On the right is a Pioneer videodisc player (with an RS-232 interface) and a color monitor.

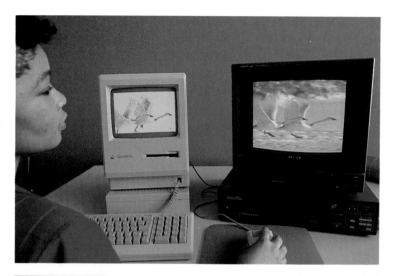

▶The Navigator card on the computer screen is one view of the table of contents. It's a cascading menu; each choice opens another set of choices.

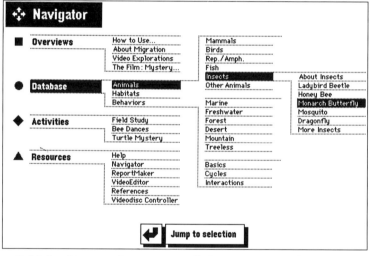

I think of it as analogous to *wayfinding*, a term used in environmental design. Wayfinding involves getting to a place you can't see. Romedi Passini, author of *Wayfinding in Architecture* (Van Nostrand Reinhold, 1984), says, "Wayfinding is the spatial problem-solving process to reach a destination. That process requires a plan of action. … Environmental communication must provide the information needed to process that decision plan."

Interactive Media

►Opening image on computer screen (left) and video monitor (right).

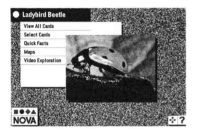

►Series of computer screen images (left) and their accompanying video images (right).

Paul's design plan had to include navigational aids. One interesting navigational technique that Paul designed was the concept of picture as background. He reversed the usual approach in print layout, where you start with white space and insert photos. Paul inserts the textual information into the image. The background picture gives the viewer a sense of where he is in the data base.

Another challenge in such a project is dealing with huge amounts of information. A piece that encourages exploration has to have lots to explore. The volume of material for Interactive NOVA was staggering. When I asked Paul how many cards there were, he started to calculate, but gave up after a few hundred.

▶Series of computer screen images (left) and their accompanying video images (right).

I asked Paul, "What was most challenging about this project?" He answered, "The overall concept, trying to think of how it all works as a unit, a unified whole. All the parts must support the general concept.

"I've come across the word *design* a lot on this project. Too often graphic designers lay claim to the term designer. Programmers and educators who do the content/conceptual design are considered designers as well. I want to be a partner to those designers, so that they can use my skills as a graphic designer. I want to be part of the concept design, and to do that I need to understand the programming and editorial intent. This is especially important in multimedia."

Then I asked Paul what was most exciting. He said, "We're finally seeing a synthesis of books and TV. When you have frame-by-frame access to multiple layers of information, you have booklike access to the audiovisual experience of television."

Appendix A

COMPUTERS. You will curse them and you will bless them. The better informed you are, the more successful you will be with your new tools. Here's a list of resources that I've built over the years. I have focused on the Macintosh environment. The telephone numbers shown were accurate as of press date.

TRAINING AND EDUCATION

You can find education and training sources at universities, service bureaus, consulting firms, user's groups, and training centers. For help finding training in your area, call the Apple Training Alliance at (800) 538-9696.

The best way to learn to use computers for design is to find a trainer who understands design. For example, Jeff Loechner, President of Mac in Design, (203) 221-1545, helped me layout this entire book.

Many of the software companies have authorized trainers. Call the software company of your choice for local training recommendations.

SERVICE BUREAUS

Chances are there's a service bureau near you, ready to take your Macintosh disk. If you want to get an idea of where they are throughout the United States, you can get the Type World Directory of PostScript Printout Services for $15. Call (603) 898-2822.

CONFERENCES/TRADE SHOWS

Most of these conferences are yearly, so if you've missed the one you want, start making your plans for next year.

Art X and Type X: (603) 898-2822

Carnegie-Mellon University: Department of Design, MM110, Pittsburgh, PA 15213

Graph Expo: (703) 264-7200

MacWorld: (617) 361-8000

Magazine Design & Production: (913) 642-6611

Magazine Publishing Congress (The Folio: Show): (203)358-9900

NCGA: (800) 225-NCGA

Seybold Seminars: (213) 457-5850

SIGGRAPH: (212) 752-0911

The New Designer (914) 741-2850

BOOKS

There are lots of books on desktop publishing in your local bookstore. You might start with these:

Desktop Publishing with Style, by Daniel Will-Harris, And Books: (219) 232-3134

Desktop Publishing Bible, by The Waite Group and James Stockford, Howard W. Sams & Co., Inc.: (800) 428-7267

The Art of Desktop Publishing, by Tony Bove, Cheryl Rhodes, and Frederick Davis, Bantam Books: (800) 223-5780

TYPE

Mactography has published a *PostScript Type Sampler* for $75. Updates are available at an additional cost. Call (301) 424-3942.

Appendix A

PUBLICATIONS SPECIFICALLY ABOUT COMPUTERS

There are tons of periodicals. (My sagging bookshelves attest to that!) Here's a sampling with phone numbers for subscription information:

Computer Graphics World: (918) 831-9400

Desktop Communications: (212) 867-9650

Graphic Arts Monthly: (303) 388-4511

MacUser: (303) 447-9330

MacWeek: (609) 428-5000

MacWorld: (800) 525-0643

Personal Publishing: (312) 690-5600

Publish!: (800) 525-0643

Seybold Report on Desktop Publishing: (215) 565-2480

Step by Step: Electronic Design Newsletter: (309) 688-8800

Verbum: (619) 233-9977

In addition, many vendors offer informative newsletters free to their registered users.

USER'S GROUPS NEWSLETTERS

Apple (800) 538-9696

EVENTS

Be sure to check for local events sponsored by your local chapter of AIGA, your local art directors' club, or design organization, and special events offered by hardware and/or software companies, local service bureaus, or computer stores.

BUYING GUIDES

One of the most useful publications I've found is *AnswerSource: The Business Sourcebook for the Macintosh*. With one page per product, it shows a product shot and a screen shot, and gives a product overview, features, ordering and support information, and system requirements. Two issues per year: $14.95. Call AnswerSource, Joint Solutions: (408) 338-6471.

You can get publications that list thousands of products; some have a listing of over 3,500.

Macintosh Buyers Guide: (800) 826-9553

MicroAge: (602) 968-3168

The Apple Guide to Desktop Publishing: (408) 996-1010

Software buyers guides that are also mail houses:

Businessland: (800) 551-2468

Egghead Discount Software: (800) EGGHEAD

MacConnection: (800) 622-5472

Worksource is a graphic arts sourcebook for the New England area that has included a section on computer-related resources. Call (617) 864-1110.

Finally, it's hard to beat the Yellow Pages.

Appendix B

I HATE ACRONYMS, don't you? Especially when you're supposed to know what they stand for. Like when the service bureau asks you questions about your very own computer–"How much RAM do you have?" or "Is your port SCSI?"–and you have no idea what they're talking about. How embarrassing!

I've listed and explained some of the most commonly used and bewildering acronyms that I've come across. The list is only a tiny subset of all the letters you're likely to hear strung together at the local MUG meeting, but it's a start.

ASCII (PRONOUNCED "ASK-EE")

American Standard Code for Information Interchange: An internationally standardized character code system that identifies computer keyboard characters: letters, numbers, punctuation, and control keys. An ASCII file has only plain text and basic text-formatting like spaces and carriage returns, but no graphics or type specifications. Standards are crucial when you're sending or receiving data from one computer to another. For example, ASCII text is the simplest form in which to get text from a client electronically. You apply typographic specifications in your own page layout program.

BIT

A contraction of "binary digit": A bit is the smallest unit of information that a computer deals with. A bit represents a "yes or no" or "on or off" choice. In bit-map characters and graphics, the bits are represented by pixels—tiny squares on the monitor that are either on or off. Let's say you have a one-bit image: that means it's black and white only. A pixel can be represented by more than one bit. The more bits you add, the more choices you have, like additional greys or colors. A 24-bit color image can have millions of colors.

BIT MAP

A graphic in which the largest element that can be worked with is an individual bit. A bit-map graphic is stored by representing each pixel (picture element) as a bit (on or off) in the computer's memory. A bit-map graphic is usually a scanned image or a graphic created in a paint program, as opposed to an object created in a drawing program (like Aldus FreeHand or Adobe Illustrator), in which lines and shapes are stored as single elements.

CD

Compact Disc: A 4.72-inch optical (as opposed to magnetic) plastic disc that stores audio in a digital format. It stores the digital information in tiny pits that are read by a laser beam. Discs are now being used to store text as well. See CD-ROM for more interesting uses of CDs.

CD-I

Compact Disc-Interactive: A computer-based system for simultaneous and interactive presentation of digital video, audio, text, and data. Like CD-ROM, the disc can't be erased or changed. The specifications for CD-I were developed jointly by Philips and Sony. You may be more familiar with the interactive videodisc, which looks like a 12-inch record. It stores analog, as opposed to digital, video. (See chapter 40, "Interactive Media.")

CD-ROM

Compact Disc-Read Only Memory: A 4.72-inch optical disc; a memory storage medium used primarily to store computer data.

Appendix B

A CD-ROM holds about 550 MB (megabytes) of data. "Read Only Memory" means that you can't erase, change, or record information, like you can on the floppy or hard discs you normally use. CD-ROM is perfect for huge volumes of reference material. It's also being used to store catalogues of clip art or stock photography. The CD-ROM disc player is connected to a personal computer. You specify what you want through the computer, which searches the CD-ROM and instantly locates and retrieves the information you're looking for.

CPU

Central Processing Unit: Usually a single circuit board in the computer that performs the calculations and data manipulations in a computer. That covers just about everything you're doing on your computer. For example, when you resize a scanned image on the screen, the CPU is performing calculations and carrying out your instructions.

CRT

Cathode Ray Tube: The screen in a computer monitor, and in your TV, too.

DA

Desk Accessory, usually seen as Font/DA: A desk accessory is a mini application on the Apple menu, and it's available no matter what software you're currently running. A desk accessory is typically a calculator, a clock, the control panel, etc. When Apple comes out with System 7, all applications should work like DAs–available at all times.

EPSF

Encapsulated PostScript File: A file format for graphic shapes and objects that contains a complete PostScript definition of a file. It can also include a bit-map equivalent for the monitor. This format is widely used for transferring images from one type of document to another (e.g., from a drawing program to a page layout program). Another format is called PICT.

HDTV

High Definition Television: A new format for television that will increase the resolution of our home television viewing. Now we watch NTSC (see below), which has 525 vertical lines of resolution. Several standards are being proposed for HDTV, which will have as many as 1,050 lines or 1,125 lines of resolution. The picture will not only be sharper, it will also be able to accommodate the wider aspect ratio of movies, unlike today's TV. HDTV development has been in the works for years; its readiness for the public has more to do with international politics and economics than with technology.

HFS

Hierarchical File System: A form of computer memory organization. You can put your files in folders, and then put those folders into other folders (directories, subdirectories, and files). You can create as many levels as you want, depending on how you like to organize your work.

LAN

Local Area Network: Hardware and software systems that connect computers together to share information like text or data base files, and resources like hard disks, printers, and scanners. The computers are joined together by a cable, and they're all within the same building.

LASER

Light Amplification by Stimulation of Emission of Radiation: Ugh! Bet you never knew that was an acronym. But it's interesting: A laser processes a beam of light through a crystal that makes the beam extremely narrow, precise, and powerful. Laser beams are in most of the typesetters and printers we use now. They're also used by surgeons in eye surgery and by hip rock concert light show technicians for lighting cigarettes.

MB

Megabyte: A unit of measurement equal to approximately 1,000K (kilobytes) or 1,000,000 bytes. (More precisely for the nerds in the audience: 1,024 kilobytes, or 1,048,576 bytes. A byte, by the way, is 8 bits. Look, it's no worse than learning about points and picas.) This term is used to describe the amount of memory (storage space) you've got, say, on a hard disk, or how much storage space a file occupies. This is important, because you have to know how much storage space you need for the files you're working with. For example, you might have a 20-MB hard disk, and think that's more than enough. Then you start loading on software and fonts. A page layout program alone takes up a good 800K of storage space. This chapter, if stored in ASCII, takes up about 13K. If I add type specs to it, it gets bigger, about 23K. Scanned color images take up a lot of space, from 250K to 1MB for a full-color, full-screen image.

MSDOS

Microsoft Disk Operating System: The operating system that's used in the IBM PC (under the name PC-DOS) and IBM-compatible computers.

MUG

Macintosh Users Group: A group of local Mac users who get together to help each other and share information.

NTSC

National Television Systems Committee video format: The color television format used in the United States and prepared by the National Television Systems Committee. Refers to broadcast-quality television. It will hopefully be replaced in this decade by something superior like HDTV.

OCR

Optical Character Recognition: Software that allows a computer to read printed text and translate it into a computer text file. Designers who can't type think this is real exciting: They'll use OCR to scan in text that their clients send. Usually this is major overkill. OCR is only useful if you have many pages of text; otherwise, you're spending several thousand dollars and having to learn the software. And OCR's not 100% accurate, and needs to be proofed anyway.

PICT

Picture Format: A format for the Macintosh for storing graphics, such as those created with MacDraw. Other programs, such as page layout programs, can read the files directly from disk, or from the Macintosh Clipboard, and therefore the graphics can be created in one program (e.g., MacDraw) and used in different programs' documents. Unlike bit-mapped graphics, PICT graphics are stored as mathematical descriptions so they can be scaled and/or printed out at higher resolutions. Another format for storing and exchanging graphics between documents is EPS.

PICT 2

An update of the basic format that includes color and greyscale information.

RAM

Random Access Memory: The part of the computer's memory that temporarily stores programs and other information while you're working with it. The data and the software are transferred from your disk into RAM while you're using them. That makes the response time much faster; if you've ever had to work with a program running off a floppy disk, you know the meaning of "tedious." You have to wait for many seconds while the computer gets the information from the disk that it needs to carry out your instructions. The more RAM you've got installed in your computer, the more data you can manipulate at one time, like scaling a color picture.

Appendix B

RGB

Red Green Blue: A type of color output to a computer monitor, consisting of three separate signals (on separate wires) for the red, green and blue components of the picture. This is additive color, the opposite of CYM (cyan, yellow, magenta), the primary colors in subtractive color mixing for printing inks. The Letraset videotape that comes with ColorStudio is very helpful in showing how this applies to actual use on the computer.

RIFF

Raster Image File Format: A file format for bit map and scanned graphics, developed by Letraset USA. This is a lot like TIFF (see below), but it's used in Letraset programs like ImageStudio. It includes color and greyscale information.

ROM

Read Only Memory: The portion of the computer's memory that stores information that you can access but can't change and you can't store more information there, either. For example, large portions of the Macintosh's operating system are stored on ROM computer chips inside the Macintosh. This stays in the computer even when you turn it off, unlike RAM.

RS-232

Revised Standard-232: A standard for the serial interface between a computer and its peripherals. This is very slow data transfer. I asked an expert how RS-232 compared to SCSI (see next item). He said it's like comparing a garden hose to a water main. You might use an RS-232 cable, for example, to connect a computer to a dot matrix printer, where you're just sending an ASCII file. (See? Now you know what ASCII means.) But you wouldn't want to use it for a laser printer where you're sending lots of data like outline fonts and graphics and pictures—it couldn't handle that much information all at once.

SCSI (PRONOUNCED "SKUH-ZEE")

Small Computer System Interface: A specification of mechanical, electrical, and functional standards for connecting computer peripherals like hard disks and printers to personal computers. You connect your peripherals to the SCSI port on your MacPlus, MacSE, or MacII. Any of these devices is referred to as a SCSI device. If it isn't SCSI, it won't plug in.

TIFF

Tag Image File Format: A document format standard for bitmap graphics, like paint graphics and scanned images. It includes color and greyscale information. Some sources say TIFF was developed by Aldus, Microsoft, and leading scanner vendors; some say Aldus, Adobe, and Apple developed it. When the TIFF images are printed, the shaded or colored pixels are halftoned.

WORM

Write Once Read Many: This is permanent storage; you can record information on a disc and read it, but not erase or change it. You start with a blank disc and store or scan whatever you want to keep—usually a data base of information that you need for frequent reference.

WYSIWYG (PRONOUNCED "WIZZY-WIG")

What You See Is What You Get: Supposedly, what you see on the computer screen looks exactly like what you get when you print it out. This capability was a breakthrough in the typesetting industry, because typesetters used to see typesetting codes and green stick figures on their computer monitors. With WYSIWYG, they, and now you, see actual typefaces and point sizes, with all elements in place. Now that we have products like Adobe Type Manager, which displays real letterforms, and color calibration tools from Radius, computer screens are looking more WYSIWYG-y.

Credits

Pages 7 through 9
Courtesy of Bitstream, Inc.

Pages 10 and 11, bottom
Courtesy of Summagraphics Corporation

Page 11, top
Courtesy of GTCO Corporation

Page 12, top
Courtesy of Measurement Systems, Inc.

Page 12, bottom
Reprinted with permission of Hewlett-Packard Company

Page 13
Courtesy of MIT Media Lab

Page 23
Courtesy of Bitstream, Inc.

Page 30
Tyler Peppel
Designed on the Lightspeed™ Qolor System
Lightspeed™ is a registered trademark of Crosfield Lightspeed.

Page 34
Nathan Felde
Designed on the Lightspeed™ Qolor System
Lightspeed™ is a registered trademark of Crosfield Lightspeed.

Pages 39 and 40
Mary Anne Lloyd
Designed on the Lightspeed™ Qolor System
Lightspeed™ is a registered trademark of Crosfield Lightspeed.

Page 44, top
Russell Brown
© 1985 Adobe Systems Incorporated. All rights reserved.

Page 44, bottom
Ronn Campisi

Pages 48 through 50
Courtesy of Bitstream, Inc.

Pages 65 and 66
Sarah Speare, SEGD

Pages 69, 72, 74, 75
Lou Jones

Pages 119 through 121
Ronn Campisi

Page 119
Photograph © 1988 Peter Jones
Illustration by Anthony Russo

Page 145
Cover photograph by Michael O'Neill

Pages 150 through 169
The illustrations in this chapter appear courtesy of Burns, Connacher & Waldron Design Associates Inc.

Credits

Pages 150, 151, 164, 168
Photography by George Disario

Pages 175 and 176
Clement Mok

Pages 181, 182, 184
© 1989 WGBH Educational Foundation

Page 184, bottom; pages 185 and 186, all images in left column;
page 185, top right
© 1989 Apple Computer, Inc., WGBH Educational Foundation,
Peace River Films, Inc. All rights reserved.

Page 185, middle right
Pam Moran

Page 185, bottom right and page 186, bottom right
Peace River Films, Inc.

Page 186, top right
H.B. Kane, U.S. Fish and Wildlife Service

Index

Page references in *italics* refer to figures.

Accounting, software for, 115–17
Additive color, 197
Adman, 116
Adobe
    Illustrator, 146, 151, 157, *158*, 163
    Type Manager, 198
Agfa Compugraphic, 168
AIGA Journal, 133
Air spring-loaded knife, 74
Aldus, 59
    FreeHand, 157, 177
    PageMaker, 59, 119, 160, 161, 182
Alphabets, using electronic rulers, 8. *See also* Characters; Letters; Type
Alphabets, Inc., 146
Altsys Fontographer, 145
Amiga, 179
Animation
    Amiga for, 179
    in HyperCard, 176–77
    MacroMind Director for, 178
Annual report design, 159–62
AnswerSource: The Business Sourcebook for the Macintosh, 190
Apple Computer, Inc., 180, 182
Apple computers, software available for, 78. *See also* Macintosh
Apple Training Alliance, 187
Artwork, scanning, 6–7
ASCII code, 191

Berlow, David, 145
Bernhard, Lucian, 145
Billing, computers and, 121, 130, 173, 174
Bit-map characters, 192
Bit-map graphics, 192
    TIFF for, 198
Bit maps, 5, 6, 192
Bits, 191–92, 195
Bitstream, Inc., 7, 70, 145
Black, Roger, 145
Black-and-white ad layout, 20
Books, on desktop publishing, 188
Boston Computer Society, 79
Brainerd, Paul, 59
Brand, Stewart, 108
Braun European Top Twenty, 177
Broderick, Peter, 104
Burns, Bob, 150, 152, 157, 159, 163–65
Burns, Connacher & Waldron, 150–70
Business management
    computers for, 115–17
    software for, 56–57, 59
Buying guides, 190
Bytes, 195

Camex, Inc., 7
Campisi, Ronn, 118–22
Captured keystrokes, 14–18. *See also* Word processing
    defined, 14–15
Carter, Matthew, 47–51
Cathey, Brad, 56–57

Index

Cathode ray tube (CRT), 193
CD (compact disc), 192
CD-I (compact disc-interactive), 192
CD-ROM, 179, 192–93
Central processing unit (CPU), 193
Character masters, in digital typesetters, 5.
   See also Digital type masters
Characters. *See also* Alphabets; Letters;
   Type
  scaling and rotating parts of, 8
  scanning, 6–7
  stored in digital typesetters, 5–6
  using electronic rulers, 8
Clement Mok Design, 175–77
Clients
  educating, 147–49
  keeping up with, 88–90
Clifford Selbert Design, 116
Cold media, 110–11
Color
  for comps, 163–65
  in desktop publishing, 159
  printers, 164–65
  resolution and, 23–24
  workstations, 20
ColorStudio, 197
Commodore, 179
Compatibility, 94–97, 154
Compressed sans serifs, 48, 49
Comps
  color, 163–65
  producing electronically, 27–28
Computer-aided publishing. *See also*
  Desktop publishing; Page layout
  software
  graphic designers and, 88–90
  user groups for, 59
Computer companies, reliability of, 83–84
Computer consultation, by graphic
  designers, 147–49
Computer graphics systems
  benefits of, 99–100, 113–14, 130,
    132–33
  buying, 92–93, 140–43
  components for, 82–83, 92–93
  costs of, 82–83
  as creative tools, 32–34, 58, 102–3

dedicated, 77, 81–84
demonstrations of, 63–67
design process and, 112–14
design studios and, 150–70
economics of, 171–74
experience and, 155–57, 160–62
limitations of, 64–67, 113, 121–22,
  130, 131–32
new media and, 103–4
productivity and, 118–19, 174
reliability of, 83–84
rental studios for, 52–54
resolution of, 23
survey of users of, 123–39
system managers for, 83
uses of, 129
Computer graphic trade shows, 21, 188
Computers
  amount spent on, 127, 129, 134–39,
    140–43
  applications of, 77–80
  backup suppliers for, 79
  budgeting for, 92–93
  buying, 42–46, 127–28,
  for business management, 115–17
  costs of, 77–78, 91–92
  customer support for, 79
  in digital typesetters, 5–6
  incompatibility of, 94–97
  learning to use, 43–45
  models owned or purchase planned,
    127, 128
  as production tools, 102
  publications about, 189
  reliability of, 78
  repair service for, 78
  selecting, 77–80, 81–84
  service contracts for, 79
  software available for, 78
Conferences, 188
Connacher, Nat, *150*, 151, 152, 159
Connect, 176
Control points, 6, 7–8
Coordinate points, on tablet, 11
Copywriters, use of word processors by,
  26–27
Corporate-identity program, 152

Corrections, to mechanicals, 35–37
Coyne, Patrick, 126
Coyne, Richard, ix, 123, 126
CPU, 193
Creativity, computers and, 32–34, 58, 102–3
CRT, 193
Crumpton, Michael, *150*, 155–56, 157, 163–65
Cursor, moving with mouse, 10
Cutting machines, for sign fabrication, 73–76
Cybermation, 70
CYM (cyan, yellow, magenta), 197

DA (desk accessory), 193
Data base programs, 116–17
for compiling survey results, 126
Dataflex, 159
DDL, 96
Dedicated computer graphics systems, 77, 81–84
Delman, Tom, 70–71
Design development, tools for, 58–59
Design management, 55–59. *See also* Business management
software for, 59
tools for, 56–57
Design Management and Computer conference (1986), 55–56
Design Management Institute, 55–56
Design process, computers and, 112–14
Design research, 157, 159
DesignSoft, 56–57
Design Source, 38
Design studios, computers and, 150–70
Design Technology Survey, 123–25
buying habits and, 140
survey results, 126–39
Desktop media, 177
Desktop publishing. *See also* Computer-aided publishing; Page layout software
books on, 188
color in, 159
graphic designers and, 88–90
limitations of, 177, 179

Devanagari, 49
Dictionary of American Music, 32
Digital type masters, 5–9
control points for, 6, 7–8
creation of, 6–8
defined, 5–6
quality of, 145
quality of typographic shapes and, 9
sign manufacturing and, 69–70
software for creating, 9
storing, 5–6
Digital typesetting
character masters in, 5
computers and, 5–6
early products from, 22
instructions in, 99
process of, 26–28
resolution and, 22–25
speed and, 9
Digitizing cameras, 27
Digitizing pucks, 11–12
Digitizing tablets, 7
Disk crashes, 60–62
Disks
floppy, typesetting from, 15
floppy versus hard, 60
making backups of, 61
Documentation, for specifications, 121
Dot matrix printers, 45
Drawing programs, 155–56

Editorial proofreading, word processing and, 15
Education, sources of, 187
Electronic pucks, 7
Electronic rental studios, 52–54
Electronic rulers, 8
Environmental design, type for, 68–76
Environmental theaters, 109–11
EPSF (Encapsulated PostScript file), 193–94
Exploratorium, 109–10
Eye movement recorder, 57

Felde, Nathan, 32–34
First Los Angeles Bank, 174
Fleischmann, Marc, 55

Index

Floppy disks, typesetting from, 15
Font Bureau, The, 145–46
Font/DA, 193
Fontographer, 145, 146
Fonts
 generic, 20
 sign manufacturing and, 69–70
Format calls, 15–16
 translation tables and, 17
 when economical, 17–18
 word processing, 14–15, 17–18
4i Collaboration, 177
Fraterdeus, Peter, 146
FreeHand. *See* Aldus Freehand

Galleys
 corrections to, 17
 paste-up of, 17
Generic fonts, 20
Gleason, Vincent, 163, 165
Gordon Capital, 152–54
Graphic arts trade shows, 19–21
Graphic design, as multimedia discipline,
 177
Graphic designers
 attitudes toward technology, 106–8,
  118
 computer buying habits of, 140–43
 computer consultation by, 147–49
 experience and, 155–57
 imagesetters and, 3–4
 pointing devices and, 13
Graphics overlay board, 179

Hafer, Robert, 61–62
Haggland, Martin, 150, 151
Hard copy, 15
Hard disks
 benefits of, 60–61
 crashes of, 60–62
 size of, 62
Hardware, upgrading, 78
Haueisen, Bill, 57
HDTV (high definition television), 194,
 195
Helvetica Compressed Series, 48, 49
Hendrix, Jimi, 154

HFS (hierarchical file system), 194
Highgate Cross & Cathey, 56
High-resolution screens, 23
Hot media, 110–11
Hot metal type, 47, 48
HyperCard, 168
 for interactive media, 183
HyperCard stack, 168, 175–76
Hypermedia, 168

IBM, Inc., 179
IBM computers, software available for, 78
Illustrator. *See* Adobe Illustrator
Imagesetters, 1–4
 defined, 1
 graphic designers and, 3–4
ImageStudio, 197
ImageWriter, 142
Imagine, 177
Incompatibility, 94–97, 154
Information stations, 180
Input scanners, 27
Interactive learning programs, 180–86
Interactive media, 180–86
Interactive NOVA, 180–86
Interactive video, 111
Interactive videodiscs, 109–10, 192
Interactive workstations, 24
Interpress, 96
Isometric drawings, 155–56
Italics, 9

"Jaggies," 22, 23
Job-tracking, software for, 56–57

Kerning, 9, 87, 89
Koh, Serena, 154, 160

LAN (local area network), 194
Laser printers, 45, 122, 154
Laser technology, 194–95
Laser typesetting, 85–87
LaserWriter, 142, 173
Letraset videotape, 197
Letterforms, technology and, 47–51
Lettering artists, specification of control
 points by, 7–8

Letters. *See also* Alphabets; Characters; Type
    cutting, 73–76
    three-dimensional, in sign fabrication,
       70–76
Letterspacing
    control of, 87
    in sign fabrication, 73
Lewis, Tom, 171–73
Lightspeed Color Layout System, 173–74
Linofilm, 48, 49
Linotron 505, 49, 51
Linotronic, 165
Lloyd, Mary Anne, 38
Loechner, Jeff, 187
Logo development, animation of, 175–77
Lucian, 145

Mac in Design, 187
MacDraw, 86, 196
Macintosh
    for annual report design, 159–62
    commissioning typefaces for, 145–46
    design applications of, 151, 152
    economics of, 171–74
    hardware for, 119
    laser typesetting for, 85–87
    ROM, 197
    software for, 59, 119
    typefaces for, 85–87
    user's groups, 79
Macintosh II, 119, 164, 179
Macintosh Plus, 119, 173, 182
Macintosh SE, 171
Macintosh Users Group (MUG), 195
McLuhan, Marshall, 110, 111
Macmillan Press, Ltd., 32
MacroMind Director, 178
MacroMind Video Works II, 178
Mac Temps, 155
Mactography, 188
Management, software for, 56–57
Manuscript, with format calls, 16–17
Market research, design and, 57–58
MB (megabyte), 195
Mechanicals
    last-minute changes to, 35–37
    producing electronically, 26–28

Media. *See also* Interactive media;
    Multimedia
    computer and, 103–4
    hot and cold, 110–11
"Media Lab, The: Inventing the Future at
    MIT," 108
Memory, 195. *See also* Storage
    RAM, 196, 197
    resolution and, 24
    ROM, 197
Mergenthaler, 49, 85, 87
Metadesign, 104
MIA Prospera, 146
Mice Type, 146
MicroColor, 151, 157, 159
Microsoft Word, 119
MIT, 108
    touch-sensitive screens, 13
Modems, 27
Mok, Clement, 175–77
Monotype Composition Company, 15
Mouse
    pointing with, 10
    trackball and, 12
    use of, 29–30, 33, 36
MSDOS, 195
MTV Europe, 177
MUG (Macintosh Users Group), 195
Multimedia, 175–79
    database, 181

Naimark, Mike, 110
National Association of Broadcasters, 179
National Park Service, 163
Navigational aids, 185
Nesting program, in sign fabrication, 72, 73
Newsweek, 145
NOVA, interactive program for, 180–86
NOVA Research, 57
NTSC (National Television Systems
    Committee) video format, 194, 195

OCR (optical character recognition)
    software, 143, 196
Outlines, for storing digital type masters, 6
Output machines, 69
Page description languages, 95–96

Index

Page layout software
  graphic designers and, 88–90
  incompatibility problems, 95–96
  storage requirements for, 195
  using, 119–20
PageMaker. *See* Aldus PageMaker
Page makeup work stations, 20–21
Pagination (page layout) video display
  terminals, 119–20
Paint programs, 192
Passini, Romedi, 184
Pasteup, temporary help for, 155
Peace River Films, 181, 182
Pen plotters, 72
Personal computers. *See* Computers
Philips, 192
Photocomposition, 47–49
Photographs, scanning, 27
PICT (picture format) graphics, 194, 196
PICT 2, 196
Pillar, 175
PixelPaint, 151
Pixels, 192
  color of, 23
  resolution and, 23
Plasma cutting tool, 73–74
Plexiglas, cutting letters from, 70, 75, 76
Plotters, 72
Pointing devices, 10–13
  digitizing pucks, 11–12
  graphic designers and, 13
  mouse, 10
  position-sensitive screens, 12
  selecting, 13
  stylus and tablet, 11
  touch-sensitive screens, 13
  trackballs, 12
Position-sensitive screens, 12
Posters, color comps of, 163–65
Postscript, 96
  EPSF, 193–194
  fonts, commissioning, 145–46
PostScript Type Sampler, 188
Powell, Earl, 55–56
Preview screens, 18
Printers
  color, 164–65

dot matrix, 45
laser, 45, 122, 154
Print quality, resolution and, 24–25
Productivity, 118–19, 172–73, 174
Proof printer, 27
Pucks
  digitizing, 11–12
  electronic, 7

QMS ColorScript printer, 164–65
Quark XPress, 163

Radius, 198
RAM (random access memory), 196, 197
Repair service, 78
Reproduction cameras, 1
Resolution, 22–25
  color and, 23–24
  cost and, 24
  discrepancies in, 156
  dots per inch, 22–23
  laser printers and, 45
  measurement of, 22–24
  memory and, 24
  pixels, 23
  print quality and, 22, 24–25
  scanners and, 65–66
  of slides, 65–66
  speed and, 24
  television, 194
  of type, 66
  of video camera images, 65
RGB (red green blue), 197
RIFF (Raster image file format), 197
Rolling Stone, 145
ROM (read only memory), 197
Ronn Campisi Design, 118
Rotating characters, 8
RS-232, 197

Sametz Blackstone Associates, 15, 17
Scaling characters, 8
Scanned color images, storage requirements for, 195
Scanners
  quality of, 142
  resolution of, 65–66

Scanning
    artwork, 6–7
    photographs, 27
    text, 196
Scitex, 145
Score window, 178
Screens
    position-sensitive, 12
    touch-sensitive, 13
SCSI (small computer system interface),
    197, 198
Sekers, Alan, 177
Serial interface, 197
Serifs, 8
Service bureaus, 187
Service contracts, for computers, 79
Sherwood, Will, 171, 173–74
Shipton, Alyn, 32–34
Showscan theater, 109
Sign manufacturing, 68–76
    computer method of, 72–76
    traditional method of, 70–71
Skopek, Daniele, 117
Slides
    from video images, 64–66
    producing in electronic rental studios,
      52–54
    resolution of, 65–66
    of screen images, 31
Slide shows, on computer screen, 175–76
Smart, 145
Snell, Charles, 48
Snell Roundhand, 48, 49
Software. *See also specific programs*
    availability of, 78
    experience with, 156–59
    limitations of, 156
    problems using, 160–62
    products used or purchase planned,
      127, 129
    upgrades of, 78, 84
Sony, 192
Souza, Paul, 181–82, 185–86
Spatial Data Management System, 108
Specifications
    documentation for, 121
    format calls for, 15–16

    for imagesetters, 3
    page layout software and, 120–21
    storage requirements for, 195
Speed, resolution and, 24
Stems, designs, 8
Storage, 195. *See also* Memory
    WORM, 198
Studio/8, 151
Style sheets, 120, 162
Stylus and tablet, 11
Subtractive color, 197
System configuration, compatibility and,
    154
System managers, 83

Tablets
    digitizing puck and, 11–12
    stylus and, 11
Technical publishing, workstations for, 20
Television, HDTV, 194
Text
    previewing, 18
    storage requirements for, 195
    word processing, 14–15
Three-dimensional images, capturing on
    screen, 39–40
Three-dimensional letters
    computer method of fabricating, 72–76
    traditional method of fabricating, 70–71
TIFF (tag image file format), 198
Tombstones, typesetting for, 154
Tom Lewis, Inc., 171–73
Touch-sensitive screens, 13
Trackballs, 12, 109–10
    mouse and, 12
Trade shows, 19–21, 188
    computer graphic, 21
    graphic arts, 21
Training
    cost of, 172–73, 174
    sources of, 187
Translation table, 17
Trapping, 156
Treacy, Joe, 146
Treacyfaces, Inc., 146
Tufte, Edward, 133
Turnbull, George, 38

Index

Type. *See also* Alphabets; Characters;
    Letters
  computer storage of, 66
  for environmental design, 68–76
  resolution of, 66
  for sign systems, 68–76
Type design, 47–51
Typefaces
  alterations in, 9
  changing on screen, 27
  commissioning, 144–46
  compatibility problems, 96
  for Macintosh, 85–87, 144–46
  producing with digital typesetters, 6–9
Typesetters, 1, 2. *See also* Digital typesetters
  compatibility problems and, 96–97
  format calls and, 14–15
  value of, 18
Typesetting
  cost of, 14
  from floppy disks, 15
  laser, 85–87
  preparing text for, 14
  reducing cost of, 18
  sign manufacturing and, 68–70
  storing instructions for, 69
Type World Directory of PostScript
    Printout Services, 187
Typographic House, 18
Typographic shapes, digital type masters
    and, 5–9
Typositors, 1

Understanding Media, 110
University Brink, 70–72
Updegraff, Robert, 32
Upgrades, hardware and software, 78, 84
Users groups, 79
  for computer-aided publishing, 59
  newsletters for, 189

Video, 50
Video boards, 179
Video cameras
  capturing three-dimensional images
    with, 39–40

  for creating screen images, 30–31, 33,
    38–40
  resolution of images created with, 65
Video design, benefits of, 99–100
Video digitizers, 179
Videodiscs, 109–10
  for interactive media, 183
Video display terminals
  pagination (page layout), 119–20
  preview screens, 18
VIP machines, 49

Waldron, Jim, *150*, 152, 155–56, 159–62,
  168
Waters, John, 55
Wayfinding, 184
Wayfinding in Architecture, 184
WGBH Educational Foundation, 117,
  180–82
Will Sherwood Advertising, 171, 173–74
Wojcicki, Ann, *74, 75*
Word processors
  composing text on, 26–27
  format calls, 14–15, 17–18
  preparing text with, 14–15
Word slides, producing in electronic rental
    studios, 52–54
Word spacing, control of, 87
Worksource, 190
Workstations
  for black-and-white ad layout, 20
  color, 20
  computer graphics, 23
  creativity and, 102–3
  interactive, 24
  page makeup, 19–21
  quality of, 20–21
  rental studios, 54
  for technical publishing, 20
  tools of, 29–31
WORM (write once read many), 198
Wurman, Richard Saul, 180
WYSIWYG, 198

Youngblood, Gene, 104

Printing and binding:
Arcata Graphics/Kingsport Press

Layout and Production:
Aldus PageMaker 3.02 Color Extension
Adobe Type Manager
Macintosh II computer

Color separations:
United South Sea Graphic Co., Ltd.

Typography:
PageWorks, Cambridge, Massachusetts
12.5/14 Lapidary 333 (Bitstream, Inc.)
Bernhard Modern (Bitstream, Inc.)
Rockwell Condensed (Monotype Corporation)
Grotesque Light Condensed (Monotype Corporation)
set on the Varityper 4300P PostScript imagesetter

Design:
Ronn Campisi

Layout:
Jeff Loechner